TREASURES OF THE KING

ALEC MOTYER

TREASURES OF THE KING

PSALMS FROM THE LIFE OF DAVID

ivp

INTER-VARSITY PRESS
Norton Street, Nottingham NG7 3HR, England
Email: ivp@ivpbooks.com
Website: www.ivpbooks.com

First published 2007

British Library Cataloguing in Publication Data
A catalogue record for this book is available from the British Library.

ISBN 978–1–84474–193–9

Set in Dante 10.5/13pt
Typeset in Great Britain by CRB Associates, Reepham, Norfolk
Printed and bound in Great Britain by Ashford Colour Press Ltd, Gosport,
Hampshire

Inter-Varsity Press publishes Christian books that are true to the Bible and that
communicate the gospel, develop discipleship and strengthen the church for its
mission in the world.

Inter-Varsity Press is closely linked with the Universities and Colleges Christian
Fellowship, a student movement connecting Christian Unions in universities
and colleges throughout Great Britain, and a member movement of the
International Fellowship of Evangelical Students. Website: *www.uccf.org.uk*

Contents

Abbreviations

AV   Authorized Version
NASB   New American Standard Bible
ESV   English Standard Version
NKJV   New King James Version
RV   Revised Version
NRSV   New Revised Standard Version
$\sqrt{}$ The root form of the Hebrew verb in question

To the treasured memory of
Roy Howard Lucas
1930–2006

Preface

These studies were first prepared for the 1988 Spring Session of the Wednesday morning Bible fellowship at Christ Church Westbourne, where I was then privileged to minister. The debt I owe to that Church cannot be measured. It is a delight to be reminded in any way of those halcyon days.

The thought that these Psalms studies might become a book was planted in my mind by my son Stephen, and I have enjoyed and profited by revisiting and writing up these old friends. The pleasure has been increased by the knowledge that I was working for the Inter-Varsity Press, and would receive the direction, advice and care for which that Press is deservedly a by-word. I would like to say a particular word of thanks to Mrs Kate Byrom, a Commissioning Editor of IVP, and, through her, to others at the Press to whom the production of this book owes so much.

May the God of all grace be pleased to use their work and mine to bring every reader to deeper enjoyment of his Holy Word!

Alec Motyer
Poynton, Cheshire
2007

Introduction

The poetry of the Hebrew Bible has nothing that compares with English 'narrative verse'. When Lord Byron informed us that 'the Assyrian came down like a wolf on the fold', that's all there was to it, an elegant record of fact, decked out in somewhat improbable imagery. The poets of the Old Testament, and David among them, showed no interest in such recording of facts. When they traced the course of history (e.g. Psalms 78, 105 and 106), it was in order to assert truth, to draw out meaning, and to apply lessons. It was poetry as prophecy, a forth-telling of the truth about God.

Take Psalm 78, for example. In two parts it traces the story of Israel: from Egypt to the wilderness (verses 12–39), and from the wilderness to the Promised Land (verses 40–72). It is full of facts, but the purpose is always to bring out what the facts mean, to use them to declare 'the praises of the LORD' (verse 4) and to make them into a lesson to be passed on from generation to generation (verses 5–6), in order to hold them to the highest ideals of spiritual devotion (verse 7 onwards).

There are fourteen psalms of David that their headings relate to incidents in his life (as, e.g., Psalm 51).* They do not record those incidents; indeed, for the most part, they do not make any plain reference to them. They are, in fact, David meditating on, and drawing out the lessons from, his experiences, telling the 'story within the story', the feelings behind the facts, the way faith came to the rescue, prayer was made and heard, and, above all, the glory of the Lord in power and mercy. They are David's 'real' account* of his life story, his autobiography. They tell 'what the Lord has done for my soul' (Psalm 66:16).

It is perhaps worth mentioning that in the Hebrew text the psalm headings are not separated from the rest of the psalm, as has become the fashion in English versions. In our Bibles, the tiny print, and the way the headings are thus given a separate position, suggest that they are possibly optional extras. Indeed, it has even been known for them to be omitted altogether! Not so! We know of no Hebrew text from which they are missing, and when the text was divided up into verses, the headings were counted as the first verse(s) of the psalm in question.

If, therefore, we wish to deal straightforwardly with the sacred text as we have received it, the headings must be treated with equal seriousness. They are venerable and authoritative introductions to the psalms in question, and aids to our understanding of them. So this is what we are going to attempt.

For the most part, the psalm headings make a clear link with some recorded episode in the history of David as found in the books of Samuel and Kings (e.g. Psalms 3 and 59). Where the reference is unclear we must pursue the correct interpretation as best we can. Psalm 7 refers to an otherwise unknown incident, and, for example in Psalms 30 and 142, different settings are possible. It is also only right to point out that many interpreters would regard the headings as much later additions to the psalms, and with dubious (if any) value for understanding the psalms to which they are attached.

This attitude – and the principle on which it is based – do not appeal to me. Even if the headings could be proved to be 'late' (which cannot be done), we would still owe it to the ancient editors who put them there to assume that they did so intelligently and not in a moment of aberration! On the contrary, however, I find them perceptive and illuminating. I see no reason to suppose their presence is due to any other than David himself, and I invite you to join with me in enjoying the psalms in this light.

---

* Although the authorship of one or two of these psalms is debated – by others, not by me – for the purposes of this book they are taken to be psalms of David.

1 A tale of two kings: David and Saul

Background reading: 1 Samuel 9 – 11; 13; 15 – 17

Saul had almost everything going for him when he became Israel's first king. He could not have been more confident of God's call to him – not only the words of Samuel and the confirmatory signs, but (surely) some inward intimation of the work of God in his heart, the evidence of the casting of lots before God, and huge popular acclaim. In addition he was notably tall, something by no means negligible in a leader, and he knew intuitively when to hold his tongue, and when to do nothing. As his history develops we see how easily he attracted loyalty, so that it is not for nothing that he has been described as 'the beloved leader'. The background to this 'tale of two kings' (see the Bible references above) will repay careful reading.

The tragic defect

But there was a worm in the bud. Saul was chronically insecure. Picture this oversized fellow hiding himself under the collected bags and parcels of the assembled people! And like all insecure people he could be astonishingly decisive, but, again like all the insecure, his powers of decision could also deteriorate into silly – even sinful – impulsiveness (see 1 Samuel 22:18–19). Likewise, his genuine devotion to the Lord (1 Samuel 28:3) could degenerate into absurd religious scruples (1 Samuel 14:24). Saddest of all, his insecurity became a persecution complex (1 Samuel 22:7–8), amounting to a mania – and eventually concentrated its fury on David.

The collapse of Saul's kingship came in two stages, both of them failures to obey the Lord's word. First, among the signs Samuel gave him in confirmation of his kingship, there was the command to wait at Gilgal for seven days till Samuel should come and offer the sacrifices and give Saul instructions. Like every word of the Lord, this was seriously meant, and no doubt Samuel gave it the same solemnity and emphasis that would have accompanied everything he said in the memorable interview. Saul should have understood it so – his behaviour in the event showed that he did so understand it. But he did not obey the command, and in consequence lost the privilege of founding a dynasty: there would be no 'house of Saul' reckoned among the kings of Israel (see 1 Samuel 13:7–14 for the full story).

'To obey is better'

Chapter 15 of 1 Samuel records Saul's second failure in obedience. He was commissioned to exact the Lord's vengeance on the Amalekites,[1] and because he failed to do so he lost his personal divine recognition as king. Thus he was doubly disowned: first, no heirs and successors on the throne; then, no true kingship at all. From now on it was downhill all the way. Saul's potential was immense; his failure pitiable and tragic; the path from potential to failure was disobedience to the word of God.

Here comes David

The scene is set, therefore, for a tense conflict – of personalities, gifts and achievements – when David arrives on the scene. On the one hand, an insecure king doubly soured by failure; on the other, a youthful, assured and endlessly gifted aspirant.

With Saul's second rejection, affirmed in 1 Samuel 16:1, the Lord took steps to secure the continuation of the monarchy outside Saul's family, and the divine choice fell on the house of a Bethlehemite named Jesse. Between the lines of this famous story we can sense the growth of a police state. In a classic example of 'shooting the messenger', Samuel was by now persona non grata and had to watch his step. He needed a cover story to visit Bethlehem – and even so the arrival of such as he could have boded ill for the town, the elders fearing that they would be tarred with Samuel's brush and put on the king's blacklist – what we would call 'guilt by association'.

David was Jesse's eighth and youngest son, and was apparently somewhat looked down on by his own family because of his reputation for seeking repute by brash and foolhardy acts (e.g. 1 Samuel 17:28f.) – typical of the way in which a talented youngest son in a family of large men might feel he had to fight his own corner!

Musician and fighter

At any rate, David was the Lord's chosen king, and, from the moment of his secret anointing, was filled with the Holy Spirit. But as the Spirit came upon David so he 'departed from Saul', to be replaced, judgmentally, by a manic spirit, which could only be soothed away by the therapy of David's harp. Thus David became a member of Saul's court, though not a permanent fixture, since 1 Samuel 17:15 literally says that 'David was going and coming back from attendance on Saul to shepherd his father's flock at Bethlehem'.

This is where we find him at the outbreak of the Philistine War.

The story of David's scintillating victory over the giant Goliath – a man, incidentally, not all that much taller than Saul, who did not risk single combat – contains one strange feature. Saul had sent for David by name, and 'loved him greatly', yet, it would appear, in 17:55, seems not to know him! In one way we could explain this simply by recalling that the 'great ones of the earth' are not noted for recalling too much about the lower forms of life around them, and no doubt Saul's illness would have increased the self-centredness that often goes with high office, and might explain his failure to keep up with the 'who's who' of court life. This is a sensible and practical explanation, but not the true one. We need to note exactly what Saul asked Abner: not 'Who is this lad?' but 'Whose son is he?' That's the point. The implication is that Saul had caught wind of Samuel's visit to Bethlehem, and of the secret anointing. Was one of the elders a royalist 'mole'? Very likely. Saul's suspicions were suddenly roused about this bonny youthful champion. Somewhere in the depths of that poor, warped royal mind, was there a recollection that someone had once said 'son of Jesse'?

The 'marked man'

Now look forward to chapter 18:8, where David's conquests in battle put Saul's in the shade. We should not be surprised that Saul was jealous of the high praise heaped on David, compared with his own meagre plaudits (which, in fact, he hardly deserved – and he surely knew it); but what is surprising is that he saw David as a threat to himself and a potential replacement as king. Saul put two and two together to make an extremely troubling four, and 'kept an eye on David from that day on'. David had become the marked man!

When we sense the 'bitchy' atmosphere that now pervaded Saul's court, with courtiers ready to win in the rat race at any cost, the scene is set for the first of David's autobiographical psalms.

Notes

1 Compare Exodus 17:8–16; Deuteronomy 25:17–19.

Psalm 7

2 A good conscience in a bad time

Background reading: 1 Samuel 18 – 19

After the Philistine War of 1 Samuel 17, David became more of a permanent fixture at Saul's court, first as 'master of the king's music' (18:10) and then as the (all-too-successful) commander of an anti-Philistine task force (18:30). But the king's crazed suspicions quickly turned to enmity (18:9, 11, 29), and there were enough sycophants at court to make sure that the pot of royal hostility was kept well stirred.

The Bible leaves us in no doubt how serious sins of speech are. Isaiah knew that 'unclean lips' doomed him before the holy God (Isaiah 6:3–5). The tongue, says Psalm 34:12–13, is the key to the good life, and 1 Peter 3:10 endorses this. James 3:2 not only sees purity of speech as the mark of the perfect person, but, intriguingly, depicts the tongue as a sort of master switch on the switchboard of our lives: control the tongue and be able to 'bridle the whole body'. Not only so, but words have a dreadful power to minister hurt to others. Proverbs 26:2 sees our words as like flying birds. They will 'come home to roost', as we say, though where nothing has been done to provoke the harsh words there is no reason to fear them. But the implication is that the tongue has real power to inflict harm.

This is the setting that the heading of Psalm 7 proposes. David felt himself to be under threat from 'the words of Cush'. Typically of all the psalms whose headings refer to times or incidents, Psalm 7 contains no reference to Cush or to his hostile, malevolent words, but there were many occasions during Saul's manic pursuit of David where yes-men would have been all too ready to stoke up the royal paranoia. King Saul was himself a Benjamite, and surrounded himself with Benjamites (1 Samuel 9:1; 22:7). It certainly cannot be far wrong to link the psalm with the early days of Saul's hostility, when David's increasing popularity cannot have pleased everybody either, and, without a doubt, the king's ear would have been receptive of anything to David's detriment.

Faith first ... and second ... and third

At all events, whether from Cush's words or from Cush's deeds, and whether in Saul's court as described in 1 Samuel 18 or at some later time, David was under threat, in danger as from a rampaging lion, and bereft of human help (verse 2). The very fact that he does not particularize either about Cush himself (who is only mentioned here) or about what he said or did, means that his psalm deals with all such situations in principle. In a word, he offers us a recipe for the dark day, against any and every threat, and an antidote to a numbing sense of isolation.

(1) Faith affirms (verse 1a)

The great cry 'O LORD my God' is where the counter-attack against enmity, verbal assault and loneliness starts. It reflects David's understanding of God, and it reveals how he met this new and threatening situation immediately by a renewed profession of faith. 'LORD' (with four capital letters) is the way most English versions represent the divine Name, Yahweh, in this way following the mistaken ancient scruple that the name was too holy for human lips. If the Lord says we may call him by his name – and that he wishes so to be called (Exodus 3:15) – why should we make a virtue of cutting off our nose to spite our face by refusing to do so?

As a word, 'Yahweh' is an imperfect tense of the verb 'to be', which in Hebrew goes beyond simply expressing 'existence' to indicate 'active presence'. He is 'the Actively Present One'. However, he revealed the meaning of this name through Moses and the exodus, defining himself as the God who delivers and redeems his people and overthrows his enemies, the God of salvation and judgment.[1]

The LORD is fully, truly, completely divine. Furthermore, he is 'my' God. In contrast with the lapse of faith that loses sight of God in times of trouble, wonders if he is still there, and questions his sufficiency and almightiness – and all the other things that shake our hold on him – David looks steadily up and says, 'My God' (compare Psalm 22:1). In the thick of all this trouble God is here – present in all his divine nature, active, saving and judging. He is not a false god like Baal, who is not there when you need him (1 Kings 18:27); he is the living God; the God of NOW, sufficient for every eventuality in his fullness of deity – and, while the storm still rages, the object of David's personal faith: 'My God'.

(2) Faith shelters (verse 1b)

After this opening affirmation the Hebrew proceeds, 'in you I take refuge'. The verb is in the perfect tense, expressing a fixed state of affairs, past, present and future. It would be something of a paraphrase, but it would get the picture straight, to say, 'In you I am safe.' In other words, we need to be careful about the translation 'take refuge', for David is describing not so much an action taken in the face of danger as a situation of shelter and protection from which he looks out upon the danger that now threatens. Jesus implied the same truth for every believer when he said that 'no one can snatch them out of my hand' (John 10:28) – that's where we are; it's where we were when the trouble came and the blow fell; it's where we remain while the trial lasts; it's the perspective, or 'take', we have on life. We are a protected species, and, come what may, we live in this secure enclave.

This is not, of course, to say that we necessarily *feel* like that. David did not feel the security of the divine wall around him. He felt vulnerable, exposed – otherwise, why should he expect, any moment, to be torn in pieces as by a lion (verse 2)? No, but he knew the security was there, and that this was the 'real truth' about him in any time, place or experience. Faith is not the ability to 'explain' what is happening, nor should it feel threatened by an inability to explain. Faith is a relationship with a Person whose reliability, wisdom, justice and love cannot be called into question, and who has assured us of his active presence, saving power and sheltering hand.

(3) Faith prays (verse 1c)

'Taking refuge', then, is 'faith resting' in the Lord our God when the going gets tough. Alongside this, the prayers, 'save me ... and deliver me', are 'faith running' to God as soon as the danger threatens. 'Save' asks for protection from the specific danger; 'deliver' looks beyond that to a time when the threat itself is gone. The doubling of the idea points to the total ability of the Lord to deal completely with our needs, just as the plural 'all who persecute me' implies the Lord's power, not just over the individual, Cush, but over any enmity that might occur, whatever its magnitude. Prayer leaves the whole solution to him, confident that he is able, even though the enemy is mighty ('lion'), destructive ('rip to pieces'), and beyond human ability to meet ('no one').

It is far easier, of course, not to pray – just to grumble and feel sorry for oneself, or to 'chew the fat'. Effort, self-compulsion and determination are part of the package – but all are directed to the one vital activity of the believing, sheltering soul – prayer.

(4) Conscience (verses 3–5)

We do not know whether David composed this psalm in the thick of the discomforts (and dangers) that Cush's animosity imposed on him, or whether he is looking back on it. In either case, having recalled his safety in God and the prayer he made for rescue, his next thought was the blessedness of having a clear conscience.

Nehemiah would have endorsed what David said. When he was maliciously accused of plotting rebellion, of having had himself proclaimed king, and of appointing preachers to hype up his pretensions (Nehemiah 6:5–7), he was able to take the moral high ground by a simple rebuttal: 'Nothing like what you are saying is happening; you are just making it up' (6:8). The reply of a clear conscience has enormous force.

We are, of course, dealing with much more than the way in which David meditated on his past. This is the way the Holy Spirit inspired him, for what David claimed in 2 Samuel 23:2–3 covers all his writings: 'The Spirit of the LORD spoke through me; his word was on my tongue. The God of Israel spoke.' It is the Holy Spirit who is teaching us that the best preparation for the day of accusation and opposition is a 'conscience as the noonday clear'. This should always be in the forefront of our aims and ambitions, as indeed it was for the apostle Paul (Acts 24:16).

The accusations against David were sweeping. They are spelled out in three parallel 'if-clauses' (obscured in the NIV):

> if I did this:
> if there is any deviancy in my hands;
> if I have paid back evil to one at peace with me ...
> (my translation)

David is not, of course, claiming 'sinless perfection'. He is examining himself in a particular situation and in the light of specific accusations. First, there is his conduct. 'Deviancy' (NIV 'guilt') derives from the verb $\sqrt{}$ 'wl, 'to deviate' from the right course. The 'hand' is the organ of personal action. It is 'stained' by wrongdoing (e.g. Isaiah 1:16), but David has always, he claims, acted in a 'straight' way. He has not been crooked or shifty. Furthermore, in his relationships, with everyone who would expect him to be a friend, he has lived loyally. 'Peace' is a very rounded idea. In its fullest sense it covers peace with God, peace towards others, and the inward peace of an integrated and 'whole' personality that is nowhere at war with itself – a fully rounded 'well-being' towards God and other people, and within one's heart. Here its social implication is to the fore. David has been nothing but a loyal friend.

Indeed, he has gone further than the second mile – or so verse 4b, literally understood, says. It should undoubtedly be taken as a parenthesis, and not as the NIV, NKJV and ESV have it: ' – indeed, I have delivered the one who, without cause, is my adversary' (compare RV). We read in 1 Samuel 18 and 19 that, even after Saul had tried to kill him, David still served Saul faithfully and at risk to himself, and still soothed the king's mania with his music – again, at his own risk. It is to this that the psalm refers – though in a passing, understated way. It is part of David's memory – and, indeed, part of his example to us (compare 1 Peter 2:23–25) – but not a thing to dwell on, meriting no more than a parenthesis!

The final element in the seriousness of David's self-examination is that he is ready to accept responsibility should any charge against him be substantiated (verse 5) – to suffer personally ('pursue ... me', literally, 'my soul', i.e., 'me in my own person'), to accept the death penalty ('trample my life'), and to lose his reputation. The end of verse 5, in the NIV, is impossible.[2] The ESV translation, 'lay my glory in the dust' is correct (compare NKJV), i.e., to be known publicly and in a proved way to be exposed as guilty. Surely, then, we must acknowledge how hugely strong was David's determination to live the unimpeachable life!

(5) Judgment (verses 6–13)

But he now goes even further, for really serious self-examination must always recognize another and higher court and a more searching testing. Paul acknowledged that, though he knew nothing against himself, the real issue was that 'it is the Lord who judges me' (1 Corinthians 4:4), but, even so, David holds that he has so consistently pursued the righteous life, and in the present matter is so confident of his faultlessness, that he is ready for God's final judgment to be brought in there and then.

Contrasts

The calls to the Lord to 'arise ... rise up' (literally 'lift yourself up ... awake ...', verse 6) imply a contrast between the present and the future. As things are, the Lord often seems inactive in the face of evil, even indolent and asleep, but the coming day of judgment will reveal a very different God. Then he will get up all too evidently against his foes; he will lift himself up to overawe and dominate, and, if now he seems asleep, this will be seen as an astonishing patience and self-restraint.[3] The present appearance of things is not the true reality. When patience has had its day, the end (verse 9) will come.

As so often when the day of judgment is envisaged, the individual and the universal are held together. The issue is no longer limited to a set of events in the court of Saul at one particular date. The Lord is

Lord of the whole earth, and when he constitutes his court there are no exemptions. Verses 7 and 8 speak of 'peoples', but, alongside this universality, David sees his individual case brought before God – verse 6, 'my enemies' – and himself standing individually at the bar – verse 8, 'judge me'. The universal, the national and the individual are all alike in the presence of eternal righteousness.

A more remarkable contrast is made between the sword and the shield. The same Lord who is 'sharpening his sword' (verse 12) is the Most High God whom David sees as 'my shield' (verse 10). The wording in verse 10 is notable: literally, 'my shield is upon ('al) God'. The same preposition ('al) occurs in 1 Chronicles 18:7, where 'which were upon the servants of Hadadezer' means 'which the servants . . . carried'. So here, 'the Most High God is my shield-bearer', the One responsible for my protection and safety. The God who unsheathes the sword to execute judgment (verse 12) is the protective God of salvation (verse 10). The sword, the weapon of close combat, speaks of the application of divine judgment directly where it is merited; his 'arrows' (verse 13) find their mark at a distance. Together, these contrasting weapons show that there is no escape, no evading justice. The 'sword' also recalls Genesis 3:24, the penalty of sin in exclusion from the paradise of God; the 'bow' (verse 12) recalls the flood narrative of Genesis 9 – 12, which relates that, when the universal judgment had been exacted, the Lord hung up his bow,[4] but the day will come when that bow will be strung again for a similar universal day of reckoning.[5] But, in the thick of all this, the God of the sword, the bow and the flaming arrows is also the God of the protective shield and of salvation: the only way to flee from God is to flee *to* him, and David, ready to assert his guiltlessness under the present accusations levelled at him, knows that when that day comes he will need a divine shield and saviour.

For the verses make us face a truth about the God of the Bible that we would rather rewrite: the active, judgmental side of his holiness, which cannot tolerate what offends it. Taking the key words in the order that they appear, 'anger' (verse 6) is annoyance as an actually felt reaction, a personal rage; 'justice' (verse 6) is making the correct and authoritative 'judgment' or decision in a given situation. It very often means 'setting things to rights' (e.g. Psalm 98:9), but here it refers to passing and executing judgment as the only right decision to settle this particular issue. 'Judge' (verse 8) is used of having a case against someone, making out a case, bringing a case to trial, and arguing a case in court. In other words, the Lord's felt annoyance is not arbitrary but strictly within the limits of his law, and his judgment when executed is the outcome of a case stated, argued, proved and legitimate – a 'due process' of law. 'Minds and hearts' (verse 9) is literally 'hearts and kidneys'. Since the 'kidneys' are used at times in the Bible as the seat of the emotions, 'heart' (which can be used of the emotions) here refers to thoughts, imaginings – the more mental side of our inner constitution. There is nothing hidden that will not come under scrutiny and judgment (compare Hebrews 4:13). 'God ... a God' (verse 11): the first word is the plural noun, *'ĕlōhîm*, God in the fullness of the divine attributes; the second word is *'el*, God in his transcendent deity. And, finally, 'expresses his wrath' (verse 11) is the participle *zō'ēm*. Like 'anger' (verse 6) this too is a word of felt emotion; a translation like 'is outraged' catches the sense. The day of judgment does no more than make manifest and final what is an everyday reality in heaven, 'the wrath of a sin-hating God'.

(6) Understanding (verses 14–17)
Verse 14 opens with a word omitted by the NIV, the old-fashioned but very important word 'Behold' – too important to be left out (NKJV). It sets the scene for these final verses of David's meditation: 'Look at it like this', it says; 'This is the way it is.' No matter how long a period of gestation (verse 14), no matter how its origin may be described (verse 14b), the results of sin are the same.

Firstly (verse 14), sin (here *'āwen*, 'misdemeanour', sin as a troublemaker) is a falsehood, a lie – or, as the NIV puts it interpretatively, 'disillusionment'. It never does what it promises; it always results in disappointment. Does it promise pleasure? Be sure it will bring pain and remorse. Does it promise fulfilment, real life? Be sure it will shrivel up the personality.

Secondly (verse 15), sin contains within itself its own destruction. It is like digging a pit only to fall into it. This is the reality of living in a world created and run by a holy God. In the ultimate reckoning, no good ever goes unrewarded, nor does any wrong ever fail to bring the ruin that is built into its very constitution.

Thirdly (verse 16), sin is a boomerang. 'Trouble' in Hebrew (*'āmāl*) is as non-specific as the English translation. It has in mind the pain that trouble brings; it is intended to hurt someone else, but it is a boomerang, and the pain turns back on the perpetrator. 'Violence' (*ḥāmās*) is specifically harm done to another person, social calamity, offences within relationships. Boomerangs all!

But there is another side to living in God's world. His 'righteousness' is his unfailing addiction to what is right, his insistence that what is right in his eyes will come to pass. There, in the thick of trouble he has not sought, amid enemies whom he has not provoked, accused of things he neither felt, nor planned, nor did, innocent as charged, pure in heart as well as in hands, David knows that the outcome will be thanksgiving (verse 17). After all, the name of the Most High God is 'the LORD', Yahweh, the God who in righteousness judges his enemies but in equal righteousness sides with and saves his people.

Notes

1 Compare Exodus 3:13–15 and 16–17. 'God' is the plural noun *'ĕlōhîm*, and is best understood as what is called a 'plural of amplification', implying that this is no 'pretend' god but the real thing, possessing in himself every possible divine attribute and capacity.

2 The verb √*šākan* does not mean 'to sleep' but 'to settle down, dwell', here in a transitive form, 'to make to settle down, make to dwell'.

3 In verse 12 in the NIV, 'relent' refers to the Lord. ESV, 'If a man does not repent' (compare RV) is a more obvious translation and expresses the same truth as 2 Peter 3:8–9.

4 Genesis 9:13: 'rainbow' is an interpretative translation. The word is simply 'bow', his war bow, now hung up because peace has been declared.

5 2 Peter 3:5–7, 10–11.

Psalm 59

3 Getting on top of things

Background reading: 1 Samuel 18 – 19

In between playing his harp, dodging Saul's spear and killing Philistines, David seemed happy enough to marry Saul's younger daughter, Michal. She was certainly delighted to marry him (1 Samuel 18:20). Saul saw the marriage as a further step in his sick ploy to murder David (18:21). One more close brush with Saul's spear, however (19:10), tipped David over the edge. He felt he could take it no longer, and – rightly or wrongly – legged it for home (19:10–11).

It is not for us to say whether David was right or wrong to run away from Saul. As Aslan wisely remarks on more than one occasion in the *Chronicles of Narnia*, 'we are never told what *would* have happened'. Nevertheless, we can't help wondering. After all, David had been anointed as king; the king's court was surely his proper place, was it not? Furthermore, however uncomfortable his adversaries were making his life, the Lord had preserved him so far. Saul's spear had never found its mark. And the Lord had given no indication that he was changing tack!

The day came, however, when Saul and his spear became too

much, and David took to his heels and made for Michal and home. Let's not hurry to criticize him. Subsequent events revealed a real murderous intent on Saul's part, and his deadly hatred of David was now in the public arena. David may well have faced such a deepening crisis in his relations with the manic king that withdrawal was, in reality, his only course.

So be it. Psalm 59 throws no light on the correctness or otherwise of David's flight, but it adds depth and fresh perspectives to the whole situation. When we read 1 Samuel 19:10–17 (please do!), we are given only the bare bones of the situation. Indeed, we are left to assume that things happened in very quick succession: David escaped, Saul's messengers followed, Michal helped David to slip away from the house, and Saul's men carried a 'pretend David' all the way back to Saul for execution. All this accords with the way Bible history is written: we are told only what we need to know, but not necessarily all the events in detail. The psalm reveals a more protracted time span. Saul's men, says the heading, kept watch on the house. They did not come barging in but 'lay in wait' (verse 3). They came back each evening, and prowled around like dogs (verses 6 and 14). The picture is of David under house arrest: by day the watchers withdraw, and with darkness they gather for their prey, knowing that it would be under cover of darkness that David would make a break. How long, then, was the waiting time? How often did David and Michal peep gingerly from behind their curtains to catch a glimpse, if possible, of Saul's hit men, and sense their intentions?

Psalm 59 takes us inside the guarded house, and into David's innermost thoughts. We meet – should we be surprised? – not someone whose circumstances have got on top of him, but the contrary. David (with Michal) has discovered the secret of getting on top of his circumstances! Three times over, the note of 'top security' is sounded. In verse 1, David's enemies are 'rising up', but his prayer (NIV 'protect') is 'O set me on high', give me the upper hand, or, better, give me 'top security' (my translation). The matching noun comes in verses 9, 16 and 17 (NIV 'fortress'): 'you are my top security' ... 'God is my top security'. In other words, there is a place above the storm (compare Psalm 61:2), higher than the enemy can reach, secure because it's exalted. Does the foe 'arise'? God's secure place is still out of his reach!

This is possibly the greatest 'lesson' of the psalm. David takes note of God's strength, security and steadfast (or never-failing) love (verses 9–10, NIV 'loving'[1]); he sees the Sovereign One as his 'shield' (verse 11); he affirms that God 'rules' (verse 13), and in verses 16 and 17 sings of the divine strength, steadfast love, high security, and of the Lord as 'a place to flee to' (NIV 'refuge'). The point is that all these are great 'spiritual' truths; they are a high 'theology', a doctrine about God. But to David they were the practical solution to getting on top of things; they were a recipe for living in, through, and on top of even the direst circumstances. God's revealed truth is a practical way of life. 'Spiritual' truths are for every day.

Structure

Psalm 59 is in two halves, with the second half elaborating and emphasizing what the first half has said:

A[1] (vv. 1–5)
    Deliver me (vv. 1–2)
    David's innocence (vv. 3–4)
    Universal judgment (v. 5)

A[2] (vv. 10b–13)
    Bring them down (v. 11)
    Their sin (v. 12)
    Universal God (v. 13)

B[1] (vv. 6–10a)
    The real threat (v. 6)
    Affirmation: 'But you' (v. 8)

B[2] (vv. 14–17)
    The real threat (v. 14)
    Affirmation: But I (v. 16)

In summary, A[1,2] are how to pray in a time of trouble, and B[1,2] how to praise in a time of trouble.

(1) The counteroffensive to even the most violent adversity is prayer

The whole psalm is an illustration of 'Take it to the Lord in prayer' – from the very pointed intercessions of the A-sections to the simplicity of 'telling God about it' in the B-sections, all we have throughout the psalm is 'talking to God'. We would not know anything of all this severity of danger and tribulation except that David spoke to God about it. It is an object lesson in facing (and outfacing) life in the place of prayer; it is a demonstration of the effectiveness of doing so.

Asking for ourselves

The more we read the Psalms, the more we will be impressed by the bluntness and pointedness of the way they worded their intercessions. Of course, the Lord will know what's best to do, and the proper course of action can be left to him to decide. David too prayed like that, simply making a prayer like 'In your righteousness, bring my soul out of trouble' (Psalm 143:11). But, for the most part, intercessions were beamed directly at the situation and the need. The verbs in verses 1–2 are strong and plain, the wording straightforward: 'Deliver', as from opposing force; 'Protect', protective untouchability, top security, raised above even those who rise up; 'Save' from the actual danger of murder ('bloodthirsty men', literally, 'men of bloods', prepared to have blood on their hands). In verses 4–5, we meet the 'impertinent' verbs. 'Arise' is really 'Wake up'/ 'Rouse yourself', as is also the different verb translated 'rouse yourself' in verse 5. 'Bestir yourself . . . wake up' is certainly plain speaking – as if the Lord God were lying down or asleep on the job! Vigorous prayer for vigorous action!

Verses 3–4a raise a topic familiar from Psalm 7: praying out of a pure conscience. Again, David is not pleading sinless perfection, but he is asserting innocence as far as the present accusations are concerned – the 'conscience clear before God and all the people' which Paul (Acts 24:16) said was always his aim, and should be ours too. In verse 3, 'offence' is specifically the sin of rebellion – in this case, David may have had his wholehearted loyalty to Saul in mind, as well as his fidelity to the Lord; 'sin' is the thought, word or deed that 'misses the mark' of what is right. In verse 4, 'wrong' ('āwōn²), is deviancy in the heart. David therefore disavows in turn disloyalty, shortcoming and a hidden agenda.

Praying about our enemies

It is remarkable – and important to note – that David asks nothing in respect of hurt done to himself. He actually prays for the withdrawal of divine favour (verse 5, 'show no mercy/grace'), for divine action that sets a moral example to Israel (verse 11), for an exact requital in respect of sins committed (verse 12). Even when he specifies sins of speech, he says neither what the words used were nor that they were spoken against himself. Yes, he would wish their sin of arrogance – a 'lofty' attitude towards others – to be rebuked, but verse 13 shows the tendency of his thoughts, that there should be a worldwide revelation of the God of Jacob.

(2) The knowledge of God is the key to confident living and calm endurance

The NIV translates verse 5a as an address, but in David's Hebrew it is actually an affirmation (compare ESV), which we could render: 'And you are yourself Yahweh, God (who is) Hosts, the God of Israel.' In other words, before David made the appeal that we find in verse 5b, it is what he knows about God that enables him to pray with such forthrightness – and indeed to live with such calmness under stress, and to dominate rather than be dominated by events.

First of all, his God is Yahweh. We have lost so much through allowing our English Bibles to suffer the ancient scruple against using the divine name. 'Yahweh' is the personal name of the God the Bible reveals; in the Old Testament it is the name of the Holy Trinity, for the God of the Old Testament is not 'God the Father' but 'the Holy Trinity incognito'; 'Yahweh' is 'who' God is, just as the noun 'God' is 'what' he is. In days gone by, two men of any age, on first meeting, would be 'Mr' to each other, but as the relationship progressed the time would come when they would give each other the privilege of using first names. A young person would automatically call older people Mr or Mrs or Miss, and there would be a real sense of privilege and increasing intimacy when the older person said, 'Call me by my first name.' Even so, the Lord God gave his people the privilege, and the closeness to himself, of using his first name: 'This is my name for ever, by which I am to be remembered' (Exodus 3:15) – the name Yahweh. And Yahweh, at the exodus, linked his name with the mercy that redeemed his helpless, undeserving people, and the power by which he dominated, overthrew and judged the superpower of the then world, poised as it was against him and his people. David knew his God by name, and felt the confidence of wrapping that name round himself. Like Patrick so much later, he 'bound unto himself . . . the strong Name of the Trinity'.[3]

Yahweh is further described as 'God (who is) Hosts'. In most cases where it occurs in the Bible, this title, familiar in the older translations, links the two words in a genitive relation: 'God of Hosts'. Here, however, they are two nouns lying side by side, nouns in apposition, helping us to understand what the title means. Yahweh is Hosts. Within his own nature there is every possible potentiality and power. He is not a bare 'one', but a One which holds in unity infinite powers, resources, graces, goodnesses – everything that is pure and lovely.[4]

'Yahweh' points to his character; 'Hosts' to his capacity; 'God of Israel' to his covenanted commitment to the people he chose for himself. Did David feel a real thrill that he was able, in verse 1, to call him 'my God' (nkjv)? This wondrous God is mine! But much, much more: I am his! He is committed for time and eternity to me!

The unfolding of the truth about the God of Israel continues in verses 9–10a. A slight alteration of the Hebrew gives us the rendering in the niv and esv. But, leaving the Hebrew unchanged, we have an affirmation, couched as an exclamation: 'Oh his strength!!!' As we have already noted, 'fortress' here translates 'top security', the high, unreachable, protected enclave in which the Lord places his dear ones. The verse continues with 'my God of unchanging love', and says of him that he will 'go before me'.[5] 'Gloat' (verse 10b) is a particularly unfortunate interpretation of 'cause me to look upon my enemies'. The sense is a simple one, that David will be there to see the last of them and of the threat they constitute – not gloating, but outlasting their animosity. Trace the verse through, then: in the Lord there is power, protection, perseverance and providence.

Significantly, the psalm opens with 'my God' (verse 1) and ends with 'my strength, my top security, my God of ever-unchanging love'. What a surprise for the 'dogs' that came each evening, hoping to trap the escaping David. Did they see the curtains twitch and say, 'See, we've got him scared'? How wrong they were. David was not watching for them; he was watching for the God who would cause him to triumph (verse 9). And when they crept close to his house in the pitch darkness, and listened at his window or his keyhole, they did not hear the sounds of barricades going up, or of frantic preparations for flight. They heard David and Michal singing songs (verses 16–17), songs through the night and first thing in the morning, voices extolling a God strong enough for every situation, careful to anticipate every need; songs not in the minor key of lament over life's toughness, but in the major key of confidence, praise and impregnable safety.

Getting on top of things, indeed!

Notes

1 Compare ESV, 'God in his steadfast love'. God's *chesed* is his covenanted love, love resident in and arising from the will of God, his unchanging *commitment* to love us.

2 The 'parent' verb is $\sqrt{}$'*āwâ*, 'to bend, twist'. In its moral sense of 'iniquity', it refers to the sad 'warp' in the fallen human nature.

3 Taken from 'St Patrick's Breastplate', that great hymn on the Trinity.

4 Compare the use of 'one' in connection with the tabernacle, Exodus 26:6 – literally, 'and the tabernacle shall be one', i.e., a unity holding together a colossal number of individual bits and pieces. The New Testament revelation of the Holy Trinity is not a multiplication of the One God of the Old Testament, but a refocusing of the 'hosts' to reveal their true nature as The Three who are One. It cannot be said often enough that the God revealed in the Old Testament is not to be understood simply as 'God the Father' but as God the Holy Trinity incognito, the Holy Trinity awaiting his full revelation in Jesus.

5 The verb $\sqrt{}$*qādam* means 'to get there first', and here it carries the sense 'to anticipate my needs', to be there ahead of me, to meet my dangers before I do.

Psalm 34
4 An A–Z for a tight corner

Background reading: 1 Samuel 19 – 22

In the meantime, David has been on the run in a big way. When, with Michal's connivance, he slipped away from home, he made for safety with Samuel (1 Samuel 19:18), where the Lord intervened supernaturally to keep him safe (19:19–24), but, instead of taking the hint that his real security was thus in the Lord's care, David took to his heels again (20:1). In the event, Jonathan could only confirm Saul's enmity, and David resumed his lonely travels, coming eventually, via his disastrous – and duplicitous – visit to Nob (21:1–9), over the border into Philistine Gath (21:10–15).

If you are planning to visit an unfamiliar town, there is no more useful companion than the good old A–Z. It's called A–Z because it offers complete coverage, total information!

Alphabetical acrostics

Old Testament poets developed a similar form. Technically it is called an 'alphabetical acrostic', a poem in which the successive verses begin with the letters of the Hebrew alphabet taken in turn. Psalm 119 is, of course, the supreme example of this. In it, each letter of the alphabet (*aleph* to *taw*) has no fewer than eight verses to itself.

But, as always with Hebrew poetry in the Bible, the meaning is more important than the form. The alphabetical scheme is used not for the sake of artistic cleverness but as the best way to express what the poet wants to say. There are virtually complete alphabets like Psalms 34, 37 and 145; actually complete ones like Psalms 111, 112 and 119, and broken acrostics like Psalms 9 – 10. Very probably, these variations are (not evidence of damage to the original text but) aspects of the way the poets used this literary form. In Psalm 119, for example, since the author felt he had assembled all that he wanted to say, or all that we need to know, or even that can be said, about the word of God, he developed a complete 'A–Z' for our guidance. But in Psalm 145, since it would not be possible to exhaust the praises of the Lord, the acrostic is incomplete.[1]

In Psalm 34 there is no verse beginning with the letter *waw*, the sixth letter of the Hebrew alphabet, and this too is probably a deliberate intention. We can never make life's turbulences and trials fit a formula, nor can we anticipate when, where and how they will arise. Life itself is a broken pattern, and the broken acrostic reflects this.

Two ways of telling a story

So much, then, for the (fascinating) literary side of Psalm 34. What about its place in David's life?

The heading (verse 1 in the Hebrew text) refers us back to an entertaining story in 1 Samuel 21:10–15. With Michal's help, David had managed to give Saul's hit men the slip, and her subsequent subterfuge had secured time for him to make good his escape. He ran to Samuel, but, curiously, did not remain there. It is hard to resist the thought that in leaving Ramah David was wrong, for the Lord had showed his hand unmistakably in giving David all the protection he could possibly ask for. Nevertheless, David chose to go on the run again, first to Jonathan, then to the priest Ahimelech at Nob – a visit with frightful consequences – and, finally, for reasons we are not told, he slipped over the border into Philistine territory, and sought political asylum with Achish, king of Gath.

But, of course, David's cover was quickly blown and, as soon as he was recognized, everything changed. He was no longer an ordinary political refugee but a valuable hostage, a powerful 'pawn' in inter-state negotiations, something to be traded back to Saul in return for concessions and benefits. His refuge with Achish had become just as dangerous as his outlaw life, for now he was at the dubious mercy of the Philistines (compare the heading to Psalm 56).

So what is David to do? The historian in 1 Samuel tells the story in one way: David began to behave like a lunatic, running round scrawling graffiti (wouldn't we like to know what he wrote!), and becoming sloppy in personal habits – in a word, he put on an act of such con-vincing 'loopiness' that Achish took him to be mad – and therefore no longer worth anything in diplomatic bargaining: for who would want a lunatic back, or concede anything in exchange for him? Let him go!

But there is a 'story within the story'!

How David must have loved telling his story! What a laugh! Did his 'merry men' encourage him, round their night fires, to tell it again and again? Was it repeated every time someone new joined the outlaw band – and always greeted with the same roars of laughter? What a joker David was! And was there an occasion when David began the well-practised routine – 'Well . . . it was like this . . . ' – when a quiet voice said in his heart, 'But it wasn't really like that at all, David, was it?' – and in the middle of the telling David suddenly realized that the good story was not the real story at all? That it was not his clever improvisations that won his escape, but the Lord's faithfulness in answering prayer?

Such is a dramatic – but realistic – way of imagining the scene. What we know for certain, however, is revealed in Psalm 34: that when David 'wrote the incident up' in his records, it was prayer, not play-acting; it was the Lord, not David, who was behind the deliverance. Helpless as he was – verse 6, 'poor', at the bottom of life's heap – when he called, Yahweh was listening, and saved him out of all his adversities.

Read through

Here, then, is a simple outline of Psalm 34. Read it through now along these lines.

> A^1 Heading, Explanations in tension. Is David to boast of his
> vv. 1–3 cleverness (heading) or (v. 2) of the Lord?

> B^1 vv. 4–8 The Lord all around (v. 7):
> The 'poor man' called (v. 6)

> C^1 vv. 9–10 The fear of the Lord
> The blessed life

> C^2 vv. 11–14 The fear of the Lord
> The good life

> B^2 vv. 15–18 The Lord close at hand (v. 18)
> The righteous (literally, an undefined 'they'
> as in v. 5) cry out

> A^2 vv. 19–22 The real explanation: the delivering, redeeming
> Lord.

Security: the Lord is all-sufficient (A^1 and ^{2})

The psalm is careful not to discount the effectiveness of David's scheming. He really did seem mad; he really did scribble (maybe rude graffiti about Achish!) on the doors, and the Philistines really did cease to think it valuable to hold a person so plainly batty! In other words, the Bible is not careless about what we call 'second causes' – but it is emphatic that we should live all the time in touch with and confident of the great First Cause of all things, the Lord himself. If the Lord chose to make use of David's deceit to bring about his release, that is his business, part of his mercy and wholly his sovereign decision. But the 'whole truth', simply put, is that it was he who brought David out of his troubles, giving him a sure place of refuge (verses 19–22), and all the praise was due to him (verses 1–3).

It would be contrary to all we know of David to think that he lost touch with the Lord and with spiritual priorities during his time in Gath. Remember Psalm 59 and the songs that filled the darkness and met the dawn! So, here, verses 1–3 are part of the story in Gath, and the purpose of Psalm 34 is to affirm this, that the praises and prayers in Gath, not the clever dodges, were the cause of David's security and safe escape.

The priority of praise

Praise should always be the first thought. In verses 1–3 we read in turn of the *grounds* of praise ('extol', see below), its *prevalence* ('all times'), *personal commitment* ('my soul'), the welcome *effect* of praise ('afflicted . . . rejoice'), and its *goal* ('glorify the Lord').

Some of these words need a little further thought. 'Extol' is literally 'bless', the verb frequently used in the phrase 'blessed be the Lord' (e.g. Psalms 28:6; 66:20), or, as here, in a call to 'bless' (e.g. Psalm 96:2) or an intention to do so (e.g. Psalms 16:7; 145:1). But what does it mean? We understand that he should bless us, but surely it is incongruous to call *us* to bless *him*? No wonder the NIV has ducked out of a literal rendering (contrast the AV, RV, NASB, NKJV and ESV)! Think of it this way: when we ask the Lord to bless us – or friends for whom we are praying – we mean, 'Please review our / their needs and react by meeting them.' So, then, when we 'bless' the Lord we review what he is and react in awe, wonder and praise. Praise may be a response to what he does; 'blessing' is a response to what he is.

'Times' here means not a date or an hour on the clock, but a particular set of circumstances, a typical situation. 'Always' is 'constantly' and covers the time factor, constantly living with the wonder of our God before our eyes. The question therefore arises of how the Lord's praises could have occupied David under Philistine house arrest. But we are called to praise him not *for* all circumstances but *in* them. He does not change; he is still the loving, saving, caring, ever-present God that he always is; his wonderful and glorious attributes do not change. Even in the direst straits our minds can be forced upwards to review and respond to all we know of him, to all we can recall of his self-revelation, and discover freshly by reading his Word.

'Afflicted' comes from the verb meaning 'to be low', and it refers to those whom life has humbled (or humiliated), those subordinated to stronger forces or pressures, those at the bottom of the heap, the underdog, the downtrodden. Our voice of worship and praise can lift them too, and bring a joy into their trouble.

'Glorify' and 'exalt' are, respectively, 'make great' and 'lift high'. What touches the downcast and downtrodden is not so much a recaptured sense of God's glory as the realization that he is as great as he ever was, and far greater than the forces against us, and that he is as 'high' as he ever was, and far higher than even the most arrogant oppressor or adversary. In short, he is the totally sovereign Lord.

In consequence (verses 19–22), nothing can impede his power to deliver (19), hurt those who are his (20), escape his moral judgments (21), exceed his readiness to redeem (22a), or deprive his refugees of their full salvation (22b).

Promises ... promises ...

David began his psalm in a narrowly personal way (verse 1), with his own determination to fill every circumstance with praise. But it did not take him long to incorporate all the Lord's people (verse 3). His experience (verse 4) can be theirs (verse 5); they are bidden to the feast he enjoys (verse 8), and along with him are the 'saints' of verse 9 (see below), the 'children' of verse 11 (see below), and the 'righteous' of verses 15, 19 and 22, that is to say, those who are 'right with God' – the 'justified', who, like Abram, have righteousness reckoned to them.[2]

It is to these that the mighty promises of the psalm apply. Notice how the 'all troubles' at the end of the psalm balances the 'all times' at the beginning. No situation or point of time should silence the voice of praise, any more than they can defeat God's power to deliver.

But can we take seriously the extent of these promises? Not even a broken bone (verse 20)? The sad and horrific deaths of many a true child of God seem to speak to the contrary, but is it actually so? Remember that the psalmists – and the Old Testament church – had as sure a hope of heaven as we have, even if the light of Christ was yet to reveal the full truth of immortality. They too looked forward to a 'bright and cloudless morning' of song,[3] to 'glory', even though on earth flesh and heart had failed (Psalm 73:24–26), to life, joy and pleasure (Psalm 16:11), and to sharing the Lord's likeness (Psalm 17:15; the NIV has added the word 'seeing'). A book as 'earthed' and as resolutely realistic as the Old Testament cannot be accused of a flippant or cavalier attitude to life's hurts, but just as Jesus could say, literally in the same breath, that his followers would be put to death but that 'not a hair of your head will perish',[4] so the Old Testament can take the same eternal view of temporal experience. To them as to us, the knocks and bruises of earth are the weeds that have to be left there if the wheat is to come perfect to harvest.[5]

Verse 22 crowns the whole issue of our security with the double truth of redemption and no condemnation. The verb translated 'redeems', when used in its specific sense, focuses on paying whatever price the need demands. Here it is a participle, expressing the unvarying relationship between the Lord and his people; it is also in an emphatic position in the sentence, underlining what it is affirming – that the Lord who sees absolutely everything that is required, puts his hand in his pocket for the whole bill! The Hebrew verb form translated as 'condemned' is related to the noun used for the 'guilt offering'. This offering set out to deal with 'manward' as well as 'Godward' aspects of an offence by including paying recompense as well as offering a sacrifice.[6] So, then, 'redeem' speaks of the Lord's doing absolutely everything that he sees to be needed, and 'condemned' speaks of his doing absolutely everything we need. And all this is the inheritance of those who 'take refuge' in him. He is the available shelter, a place to run to, a guaranteed security.

Crying out: the Lord is near (B[1] and [2])

Part of running to him for refuge is telling him all about our troubles. The Lord whose eyes see everything (verse 15a) – and therefore he knows our needs before we ask (Matthew 6:32) – nevertheless keeps his ear open for us (verse 15b), and this can be only because he wants to hear our voices, and wants us to trust him with our needs. Whatever else prayer is, it is first of all telling God, putting needs into words.

If we take verses 4–9 and verses 15–18 out of the psalm and read them as a continuous passage, they look like this:

A^1 vv. 4–5 Prayer: its effectiveness. A testimony to experience

B^1 vv. 6–7 Crying out to the Lord, who is all around

C v. 8 Invitation to experience:
goodness, blessing, security

A^2 vv. 15–16 Prayer: its conditions. An abiding truth

B^2 vv. 17–18 Crying out to the Lord, who is near

(1) The Lord in a mobile home (verse 7)

'The Angel of the Lord' is a delightful Old Testament figure. He is not (so to speak) 'any old angel', and should always be dignified by an upper-case letter. This super-special Angel made his first appearance in Genesis 16:7–13, and what is revealed of him there reappears in other passages (e.g. Judges 13). The Angel speaks as if he were the Lord himself – and indeed Hagar acknowledges him as the Lord – but, on the other hand, the Angel speaks about the Lord as though about someone else.[7] In addition to this 'duality' of his person, in Exodus 23:20–23 'my Angel' possesses the full 'name' of the Lord, i.e. all his revealed, divine nature, and also merits the reverence and submissiveness due to the Lord himself, yet in Exodus 33:2–3, where the holy presence of the Lord would destroy them in their sinfulness, the Angel is present to accompany, lead and give victory. In other words, he is the Lord 'accommodating' (but not diluting) his holiness, in the interests of accompanying his sinful, unworthy people.

In the Old Testament, then, the Angel of the Lord is one of the indications that when it says 'the Lord is One' it does not see him as a bare unit. His oneness is the unity of a rich diversity – the Angel of the Lord, the Spirit of the Lord, the Word of the Lord – within the one divine nature.

In the New Testament, this diversity of the divine unity comes into focus as the Holy Trinity, Father, Son and Holy Spirit, the One God in Three Persons. Also, looking back, we see the Angel as a preview of the Lord Jesus Christ, in whom the fullness of God has come to dwell with us sinners. Finally, in relation to David, as he looked back to his dark, danger-filled days in Gath, he realized that the Angel had been there with him, the Lord in all his fullness, present, accompanying and safeguarding the unworthy. And not only in Gath but always, for the Angel lives in a mobile home – a tent, not a static house – precisely so that he can always be on the move as the guardian of his people.

(2) The Lord as our next of kin

Corresponding to the Angel (verse 7), we read that 'The Lord is close' (verse 18). This is a correct translation of *qārôb*, but the word also has a semi-technical use for the closest relatives, the next of kin. In Leviticus 21:2, for example, a priest is not allowed to go into mourning except for, literally, 'his flesh (i.e. blood relatives), the nearest to him – his mother and his father . . . '

Leviticus 25:25 refers to the 'kinsman-redeemer', the *gō'ēl*, a sensitive Old Testament provision for times of need. Should an Israelite fall on hard times, and be at risk of having to sell his inheritance, the *gō'ēl* has the right to step in and shoulder the debt as if it were his own. The Old Testament takes all this vocabulary – and thinking – into its theology. The Lord is our supreme *gō'ēl*; he has made himself our 'kinsman-Redeemer', our next of kin indeed – and not only in the sense of closest relationship, but also in that he accepts the right to step into our need and take it upon himself as if it were his own. The verb in verse 22 ($\sqrt{pādâ}$, 'to ransom, pay the redemption price') takes the pattern one step further: so to say, the Lord will 'spare no expense', he will go the whole way, at whatever cost to himself, to discharge the responsibility of the next of kin Redeemer.

(3) The Lord who answers prayer

The overriding emphasis in verses 4–7 and 15–18 is the open door and total effectiveness of prayer as the solution to even our most threatening needs. Prayer is 'seeking' (verse 4), 'looking' (verse 5), 'calling' (verse 6); it is (literally,) a cry for help (verse 15), a 'crying out' (verse 17), and it finds the Lord's ear open (verse 15), and he himself ever listening (verse 6, 'heard' is a participle, an unvarying attitude; so also in verse 17). Prayer brings 'deliverance' (verse 4) and 'salvation' (verse 6), the former referring to the danger inherent in the situation, and the latter to the risk to the subject. 'Calling' (verse 6) is here a general word for prayer and worship, but 'cry out' (verse 17) is 'shriek', 'cry out in terror or panic', and, like 'cry for help' (verse 15), exemplifies the great biblical truth that we can actually bring our needs, terrors and feelings of helplessness to the Lord, and find that they actually commend us to him – as indeed the 'poor' man, the downtrodden one, who found that life and people had 'got on top of him', experienced (verse 6), or those whose days were dark (verse 5), and those who had no resilience, no 'gusto', left to face life (verse 18). Prayer brings us into the securest of all places of refuge (verses 8, 22).

Alongside this open door of prayer, David observes that there are conditions for effective praying. He notes persistence, using the typical Old Testament idea of 'seeking' the Lord – not, of course, looking for someone who had been mislaid, but assiduously and regularly coming to the place where, or, as here, resorting to the means *whereby*, the Lord is known to be 'found'. In verse 15 it is the 'righteous' whose cry is heard – that is to say, those who are 'right with God', but the implication of verse 16 is clear: those who are right with God are expected to shun evil – to live a life consistent with their righteous status before the Lord.

Prayer is effective for 'me' (verse 4), for all (verse 5), for each (verse 6); in relation to apprehension (verse 4), to surrounding and inner 'darkness' (verse 5), and to external circumstances (verse 6). It is true for those who persevere ('seek', verse 4), look (verse 5), and call (verse 6).

Yet it is not prayer as such that is effective, but the Lord who answers prayer.

(4) The fear due to the Lord

David, as the jovial extrovert that he was, recorded with glee that his goofy play-acting secured his safety; but David, as the man after God's own heart,[8] came to realize that the deliverance was due not to human ingenuity but to divine prayer-answering. This, as we have seen, is the storyline of his psalm. He gets to it as quickly as possible (verses 4–7) and returns to it in verses 15–18. In this way, meeting problems with prayer and finding that prayer is answered is the 'meat' of the psalm, but it is not the centrepiece.

Seeing the structure is so important in our study of the Psalms. The beginning and ending of this psalm teach us the 'brackets' within which life is to be lived in this or that circumstance; if a thought is repeated (like the truth about prayer here), it is deliberately done, driving home the truth with two hammer blows; if something lies at the centre of the psalms it is because it is of central importance – and here the truth on which David centres his meditation about the Gath episode is 'the fear of the Lord' (verses 9–10, 11–14). Surely David is implying that if only he had had a lively sense of the fear due to the Lord – instead of his panicky fear of Achish – he would have reacted and acted differently. If only he had lived with the fear of the Lord before his eyes he would have had a proper perspective on his difficulties, and a correct idea of how to behave in the thick of them. This is what we find in verses 9–10 and 11–14.

Saints and children

In verses 9–10, then, the fear of the Lord is the proper attitude of 'his saints'. The word used here has a basic meaning of 'to be separate / intrinsically different'. In Genesis 38:21–22 the NIV offers 'shrine prostitute' as a translation of *qĕdēšâ*, 'holy (woman)', and this illustrates the point: she was called 'holy' because she was separated off for the service of some god – a god whose character required that sort of devotion. By contrast, the Bible teaches that the Lord's holiness is moral.[9] Biblical holiness, therefore, is obedience to the Lord's commands, a deliberately cultivated likeness to the Lord, covering every aspect of life;[10] holiness of the hands, the tongue (Psalm 15:4), the heart – in a word, what the New Testament would sum up as 'Christ-likeness', the holiness of obedience to the word of God.

In verse 11 the NIV has added 'my' before 'children', but this offends the parallelism with 'his saints' in verse 9, which rather requires 'you his children'. In other words, the 'positional' word 'saints' means that he has separated us off for himself, but, much more, he has made us members of his family, his children. As 'saints' we are to live out our separated status in the distinctive life of obedience; as 'children' we are to live out our participation in the divine nature in imitation of our Father.

It goes without saying, of course, that those who are 'right with God' do not fear him with the craven fear of a subject cowering before a tyrant, but with a child's reverential concern to please such a loving father.

When we belong to the Lord's sphere of reality, we come under his care and provision (verses 9b–10). As our lives are orientated on him ('seek' is a participle, an unvarying attitude), so he sees to our needs. Though even the most potent physical abilities can prove a failure (verse 10a), the Lord never fails those who are his (verse 10b). Since, however, we are not only his 'saints' but also his 'children', another aspect of life comes to the fore. Just as we say to new parents, 'Is the baby talking/walking yet?', so the Lord expects his children to develop actively in holiness, to set themselves to learn the fear of the Lord (verse 11a), to cultivate godly desires (verse 12), to discipline their tongues (verse 13), to take their behaviour in hand both to purge out the bad and to import the good (verse 14a), and actively to pursue that wholeness of life towards God, towards others, and within the self which is the Bible's idea of 'peace' (verse 14b).

A particular objective

It is thoroughly in keeping with the Bible's priorities that the one specific target we are to aim at in our pursuit of the Lord's holiness is the controlled tongue (verse 13).[11] But also it is no surprise to find it given prominence here. We can imagine what sort of nonsense, half-truth and downright deceitfulness may have passed David's lips as he fooled around in Gath getting on Achish's nerves! The psalm is his way of saying, 'Never again!' In addition, the call to prayer, which is the strongest theme in Psalm 34, itself requires a parallel call for holy speaking. 'Guard thou the lips from sin, the hearts from shame, that in this house have called upon thy name', wrote John Ellerton in his hymn 'Saviour, again to thy dear name we raise'. Was he not right to learn from James (3:2–12) that there is a profound dislocation in the personality if the same tongue voices blessing and cursing?

There is a true use of the tongue: the voice of praise, finding delight in the Lord no matter what the circumstance (verses 1–3), and there is a proper reaction to even mortal threat – not the reaction of self-reliance and clever deception, but flight to the one place where sure refuge is on offer (verses 8b, 22b).

Notes

1 It is made complete – in my opinion, mistakenly – by the NIV, which inserts verse 13b.

2 Genesis 15:6; Romans 4.

3 Isaiah 26:19.

4 Luke 21:16–18.

5 Matthew 13:28–30, 40–43.

6 Leviticus 5:1–19.

7 Compare also Exodus 14:19 with 13:21.

8 Acts 13:22.

9 E.g. Leviticus 20:26; Isaiah 6:3–6.

10 Leviticus 19:2–37.

11 Compare Matthew 12:36–37; Romans 3:13–14.

Psalm 56

5 'When I am afraid ... I will not be afraid!'

Background reading: 1 Samuel 13 – 14; 17; 21; 27

David's house arrest and near-death experience in Gath made a deep impression on him and lived on in his thoughts.

What lies at the heart of effective praying?

Psalm 34 resulted from David's revising and refocusing his understanding of what it was that kept him safe and opened the door for him to escape when he was in peril at the court of Achish. Oh yes, indeed, he had been such a clever, resourceful chap! And no doubt, with hindsight, when the same David was hammering them in battle (2 Samuel 5:17–25), the Philistines must have been kicking themselves for having been taken in by his acting the madman. Just think! They had him in their grasp and they let him go!

But that was not the real story. The real story was much simpler and much less entertaining, and David – in that openness of heart and mind that makes him so endearing – would not have hesitated to give all the glory to the Lord. No, it wasn't his own resourcefulness and cleverness. It was laying hold on divine resourcefulness in prayer.

Psalm 56 exemplifies the prayer he prayed, the effective prayer that brought him freedom, and transformed the sentence of death (verse 6) into the light of life (verse 13), and turned pursuit by their enemy (verses 1–2) into the pursuit of holiness (verses 12–13).

Take a walk through Psalm 56

The heading[1] takes us further into David's experience in Gath. When he was recognized he was put under some sort of restraint, expressed here by 'seized' or 'held'. The verb is not used of imprisonment, but it indicates that David was no longer a free agent. 1 Samuel 21:13 says that he was 'in their hands'. He was in fact in double jeopardy: it's likely that the Philistines' first thought was to trade David back to Saul as part of a bargain in their favour, for Saul was proving at the time to be quite a hammer of the Philistines, but, failing this, the king of Gath had his own score to settle with the killer of Goliath of Gath! David may well have thought that fleeing to Gath was something of a masterstroke, a 'double bluff'. For with his record in the matter of Goliath, Saul would surely have said, 'David will never run there'; and Achish would have said, 'David would never willingly come here.' But, if so, the bluff backfired.

Read verses 1–2. In his emergency David turned to God. *Merciful* is 'grace' ($\sqrt{hānan}$), corresponding to the New Testament *charis*, the undeserved, unmerited favour of God. David's danger was unremitting (all day) and real: 'press their attack ... attacking' are respectively 'oppress/harass ... make war upon'; 'hotly pursue ... pursue' are both $\sqrt{šā'ap}$, either 'pant after/hound me' or 'crush me down'; 'slanderers' is rather 'those keeping a (hostile) eye on me', maybe with the added idea of spitefulness; they are many, but David begins to keep his dangers in perspective by calling them men, *'ᵉnosh*, 'humankind in their human frailty', implying a comforting contrast with God, *'ĕlōhîm*, i.e. God in the completeness of his divine attributes. 'In their pride' understands the noun *mārôm*, 'height', as an adverb. But many prefer (rightly) 'O Exalted One', a fine contrast to 'humankind in their frailty'.

Read verses 3–4. The tensions between 'when I am afraid' and 'I will not be afraid' express the heart of this psalm: the actual, practical efficacy of trust, which, says F. D. Kidner,[2] 'is seen here as a deliberate act, (undertaken) in defiance of one's emotional state'. 'Trust ... trust.' To reflect the different tenses[3] used here we could expand the translation: 'The day I am afraid, for my part to you I turn in trust. In God – I praise his word – in God my trust is fixed.' This true trust, which imparts courage and resoluteness to life, is not an unfounded confidence but looks to the God who has spoken, revealing himself in his word. Mortal man, literally 'flesh', humanity, is qualitatively distinguished from God. The eye of faith sees the truly threatening host of verses 1 and 2 in their proper perspective.

Read verses 5–6. These verses complete the first half of the psalm (see below), turning from the trust that faces up to fears to look candidly at the factors that make for fear: ceaseless ('all day') misrepresentation ('twist' – very vivid, 'they torture', i.e., make David's words mean what they want them to mean), secret malevolence ('plotting ... to harm') which presses down like a great weight (literally, 'upon me are all their thoughts for harm'). 'Conspire' is an odd translation of $\sqrt{g\hat{u}r}$. Possibly (literally) 'they attack' or 'they foment trouble'. Here Hebrew uses two verbs for the price of one ('they attack, they hide'). In this two-verb idiom, the second is the main thought and the first qualifies it: 'they hide, waiting to spring'; 'they hide, at the ready for strife'. 'Steps' is 'heels'. They plot a sneaky attack from behind. 'Eager', etc., is literally 'they stay on guard according as/matching the fact that they confidently expect (to take) my life/soul'. This is all very realistic. Following the Goliath episode David would have plenty of enemies and detractors in Gath, and they would be out for revenge as soon as word got out who this immigrant was.

Read verses 7–8. The thought of the psalm reverts to that in verses 1 and 2: David resorts to prayer. Trust reposes; prayer counter-attacks. The plea for grace for himself (verse 1) is matched by prayer for the overthrow of his enemies (verse 7). This is typical of the so-called 'imprecations' in the Psalms; they are all prayers, seeking the Lord's action, leaving all to the wrath of God (Romans 12:19). David did not fight his way out of house arrest in Gath. He left no slit throats or bereaved families behind, nor even bitter memories and a bad name. In fact, at a later date he found a welcome with Achish (1 Samuel 27:13). The 'imprecations' certainly seek the downfall of antagonists, but they do not propose or suggest taking personal revenge, nor should we read them as breathing a vengeful spirit. They seriously leave everything in God's hands, but confident of two things: firstly there is a reality of divine anger (verse 7): the Hebrew word used is related to the verb 'to snort'. In the anger vocabulary of the Old Testament it refers to the exasperated reaction of felt outrage. Secondly (verse 8), the Lord is tenderly aware of every detail of what his people experience and feel. 'Lament' seems to depend on altering the Hebrew text, which rather reads: 'As for my wanderings, you yourself keep account (of them). Put my tears in your bottle. Are they not in your record?' This is a wonderfully vivid anticipation of the beauty of Hebrews 4:14–16. Kidner,[4] perceptive as ever, notes how *nôd*, 'wandering' and *nô'd*, 'bottle', rhyme, the one suggesting the other. There is never a fluctuation of fortune or a tear, but the divine pen is at the ready to record it and the bottle to catch it.

Read verses 9–11. Note the similarity with verses 3–4. There, fear is met by trust; here, enmity is met by prayer. In verse 9, 'then' is an adverb of time: the moment of prayer is the moment the enemy retreats (compare Daniel 9:23; 10:12). 'Call for help' is simply 'call out', pointing not to what was asked for (help, compare Psalm 28:2) but to the bare fact of praying, bringing the Lord into the situation. But this involves a questionable interpretation. The Hebrew makes an affirmation: 'This I know, that . . .' Prayer rests on a great conviction, 'that God is for me', i.e., on my side. This wonderful truth leads (verses 10–11) to such a trust in the Lord that fear of human enmity is put into proper perspective – not necessarily that David ceases to feel fear but that he is confident that there is *no need* for fear. Fear is no longer the governing factor. Furthermore (verses 10–11), such a trustworthy God, a God invariably on our side, is not wishful thinking. The Lord has spoken, and faith rests on his word.

Read verses 12–13. Note how verses 1–2 dwell on human enmity in all four lines, alluding to the Lord's mercy once; verses 12–13 have four lines about God with one allusion to threat and danger. Bringing the need to the Lord in prayer, recollecting his word of promise and renewing trust in him have this great result: the danger is still real ('death . . . stumbling') but it is entirely swallowed up in the greater reality of God. But more – not just the reality of the Lord but in particular the obligation of responsive devotion (verse 12) and of walking in the Lord's light (verse 13b). Also, in this beautifully structured poem (see below), verses 5–6 and verses 12–13 balance each other. The same preposition occurs in verses 5 and 12. In verse 5, 'always plotting to harm me' is literally 'against/upon me are all their thoughts'; in verse 12, 'I am under vows' is 'upon me, O God, are your vows'. The awful 'burden' of hostility has been exchanged for the welcome 'burden' of obligation. Obedience is the clue to life and light. Vows and promises of thank-offerings made in a time of stress are not attempts to twist God's arm by striking a bargain. They are expressions of determination to make spiritual progress as a result of the experience and the deliverance granted. The vow brings us to God in a spirit of dedication; the thank-offering gives glory to God, acknowledging him as the sole author of the benefit received.

The psalm as a whole

Now that we have ambled through the psalm and noted internal links in the way it is put together, read it as a whole with this outline structure in mind:

A^1 vv. 1–2 David, the object of human hostility

B^1 vv. 3–4 The trust which counters fear

C^1 vv. 5–6 David under oppression

A^2 vv. 7–8 David, the object of God's care

B^2 vv. 9–11 The trust which issues in prayer

C^2 vv. 12–13 David under vows

Central truth, wonderful truth

We have only to look at this outline structure to see what David put at the centre of his psalm: trustful faith. It is one thing to have the faith that runs to the Lord in time of need. David exercised that faith in verse 1. It is another sort of faith that rests contentedly on the Lord while the trouble lasts – and no matter how long it lasts. It is this resting faith that David affirms in verses 3–4 and 9–11. In his fearfulness, he 'turns in trust'; alongside human hostility, his trust remains fixed, and, in verse 11, that same fixed relationship of trust is constant amid all that would still give rise to fear, Oh, yes. As David looked back it would seem that his clever, resourceful play-acting melted more and more from memory, and the Lord and restful trust – trustful resting in him – came to monopolize the foreground of his memory.

Transformation

Faith changed the whole scene. There is a beautiful little Christian song once widely sung:

> Turn your eyes upon Jesus.
>   Look full in his wonderful face.
> And the things of earth will grow strangely dim
>   In the light of his glory and grace.

There have always been people of such a 'dutiful' (and threatening!) cast of mind that they condemn all this as 'escapism' – 'real' Christians wouldn't want the world to become 'strangely dim', would they? They want to face up to it, see it clearly as it is, and resolutely go out and share the gospel. But that's not what the song meant. Sure, we need to see the world and our task clearly, but, even more, and as a priority, we need to see it in proper perspective, to judge its power, its size, its hostility in the light of the surpassing greatness, glory and beauty of Jesus our Saviour. So, turn your eyes on him!

This was the lesson the Lord taught Joshua at Jericho (Joshua 5:13). Joshua took his responsibility as commander-in-chief seriously. He went out to survey his task – and met his God. It is as if the Lord said: 'You want to have a look at Jericho, do you? Right. Have a look at me first!'

Turning and trusting gave David just such a corrected perspective. He is still in the power of Achish; Philistines – perhaps specially Goliath's family – are baying for his blood; and to escape from all this is only to return to the manic enmity of Saul and his henchmen. But what in fact are they? Poor, frail humanity, mere 'flesh' ('mortal man', verse 4), in all its vulnerability and contrast with God; and mankind (verse 11), a created entity at the sovereign disposal of its Creator. Faith changes things!

Faith and prayer

It changes our view of how things are, but, more than that, when true faith issues in prayer, the prayer of faith changes the things themselves. David is our true example. He could have indulged in the all-too-easily asked questions, but in his psalm we find no 'why?' or 'why me?' or 'why for such a long time?' or 'why now?' He went the harder way, which is also the effective way. Faith is not the ability to answer perplexing questions; faith is trustful resting in the care of a Person, who has convincingly revealed himself as the God of grace (verse 1), and who, therefore, does all things well. And prayer proved effective: as verse 9 says: as prayer was made, the enemies retreated.

The real issue

This is the lesson David learned in his Philistine escapade, the lesson his autobiographical psalms would share with us. When people say – as they unfortunately often do – that some deep sadness has made it impossible for them to believe in God, they confuse faith with cleverness, ability to unravel life's mysteries. It is not so. Faith is a relationship with a Person known to be wholly trustworthy – even when he is at the same time baffling. As ever, Isaiah put it perfectly: his thoughts are not our thoughts, nor are our ways his ways (Isaiah 55:8). Faith as such is nothing apart from a trustworthy object; prayer is nothing apart from a divine hearing ear, a loving, understanding heart, and sovereign power – in fact all the things packed into verses 7–8: the God whose power rules the world (verse 7), whose knowledge embraces my wanderings (verse 8a, see above), and whose tenderness keeps a felt record of my sorrows (verse 8bc).

Given such a God, faith rests secure, prayer is potent, and, like David in his dire danger, we are always safe.

Notes

1 In the heading to the psalm there are some things we can guess at and some we cannot explain at all. 'Director of Music', from $\sqrt{nāṣaḥ}$, to be eminent, possibly 'superintendent', 'overseer', director'. Maybe there was a Temple Director of Music who edited a hymn book containing the 55 psalms inscribed as 'belonging' to him, e.g., 31; 42; 76. 'The dove of silence in distant places' could have been the name of the tune recommended for this psalm. 'Miktam' (compare 16; 56; 57; etc.) can be given no certain meaning, nor is it clear why the psalms so entitled were linked together in this way, though, of course, it must have been clear at the time.

2 F. D. Kidner, *Psalms 1 – 72*, Tyndale Old Testament Commentary (IVP, 1973), p. 203.

3 Hebrew tenses express the sort of action involved rather more than the time of occurrence. The imperfect here allows us to see an act in progress of happening ('turn in trust'); the perfect expresses what is a fixed characteristic ('trust . . . fixed').

4 Ibid., p. 204.

Psalm 52

6 A tale of two trees

Background reading: 1 Samuel 18 – 22

Go back first, and then move forward. Before he took the desperate step of thinking he would be safe with the Philistines – talk about grabbing a tiger by the tail! – David had thoughtlessly involved the priests of Nob in his personal dilemma with Saul. It had not gone unobserved (1 Samuel 21:7), and was to have serious consequences (1 Samuel 22:6–19).

You would have to go far in the Bible to find such a sharply drawn picture of the Lord's active opposition as Psalm 52:5!

The four verbs (literally, 'pull down ... scoop up ... snatch away ... root out ...') leave nothing more to be said. On the one hand, here is the total insecurity of the one who, for whatever reason, has 'got on the wrong side' of the Lord God. Such a person has no solid strength ('pull down'), no 'hold' on place or position ('scoop up'), no continuance ('snatch away'), and no future ('root out'). On the other side of the same coin, what a picture of the absolute, sovereign power of the Lord! However 'mighty' the lover of evil (verse 1), however cutting and dismissive in speech (verse 3), his power to destroy (verse 7) cannot match the Lord's power to consign to everlasting ruin (verse 5).

When this uprooted tree (verse 5) lies prone, with its roots torn from the ground and its vitality draining away, open-eyed mockery (verse 6) will replace the awe it formerly inspired, and divine righteousness will be vindicated. But there is a different tree, a luxuriant evergreen, securely placed in the Lord's presence (verse 8a), resting confidently in his unfailing love, and with an eternal security (verse 8b) in marked contrast to the pathetic insecurity of the once dominant 'mighty man' (verse 1).

There, then, is the 'tale of two trees', the uprooted and the well-rooted, the one for lumber on the forest floor, the other for fruitfulness in the divine garden; voices of mockery surround the one, the voice of praise sounds from the other; one is for the chop, the other tended by love for ever and ever.

What can be the cause of such contrasting experiences? What can result in such contrasting destinies? And what prompted David to write such a psalm?

The ear at the keyhole

The unanswerable question is whether David was right to flee for his life from Saul's court. The danger there was tragically real. Nevertheless, David was 'covered' by the Lord's declared purpose that he would be king, and many subsequent occasions of deliverance during his years on the run proved the reality of divine care. Oh yes, the Lord could have sheltered him even in the very palace itself, and what a lot of misery – not to mention needless loss of life – would have been avoided!

But David did take to the hills and the caves, and others became entangled in the web of his misfortunes.

To catch up with the background to Psalm 52, we must backtrack a little. On his way to what he had (as we have seen) fondly hoped would be safety in Gath, David stopped off at the priestly city of Nob. We are not told why he took that route. Was it hunger? Was it that, being weaponless, he remembered where Goliath's sword was? Was it just that the road ran that way and David opportunistically took advantage of what he expected might be a friendly welcome? Whatever the reason, when he came to Nob David might well have invented the saying about being 'economical with the truth'. If that is what he thought he was doing he was self-deceived. He was a downright liar! Self-preservation is an overmastering instinct, and can make cowards of us all.

Ahimelech, the priest at the time, logically feared that a lonely and ill-equipped traveller might well be a fugitive from justice – and particularly as a person of David's national renown was unlikely to be without a protective posse. 'Certainly not,' said David. 'The king commanded this enterprise; he ordered secrecy, and my troops have an assignation to meet me' (1 Samuel 21:2, my translation). All lies! 'And, as for being unarmed, it's all because of the king's urgency' (verse 8). Another lie! And poor old Ahimelech was conned into feeding David and parting with Goliath's sword (verses 6, 9). He was tangled in David's web – not here a web of danger, but a sad and silly web of lies. David certainly should have known better than to implicate others in his misfortunes; he certainly should have known better than to make them complicit in falsehood.

Enter the unwanted listener!

Almost everything about Doeg's presence in the history recorded in 1 Samuel cries out for more explanation. For example, how did he, an Edomite, come to be part of Saul's entourage, 'a man of the servants of Saul'? We cannot say. Saul had already fought some sort of Edomite war (1 Samuel 14:47): was Doeg brought back as a prisoner, first to work for Saul and then to rise to prominence? What does 'detained before the LORD' mean? The verb $\sqrt{}$ '*āṣar* is used in the general sense of 'held back' (e.g. Judges 13:16), of some unspecified cause that stopped Jeremiah from entering the Lord's house (Jeremiah 36:5) – this would speak against the suggestion that Doeg was guilty of a religious or ceremonial offence, for he is here 'before the LORD'; the verb used of Jeremiah is 'confined' or 'imprisoned' (Jeremiah 33:1; 39:15), and this is the more likely explanation of Doeg's presence at Nob, though, of course, we do not know what he had done to be given a custodial sentence. Finally, what does 'Saul's head shepherd' mean? It is better translated as 'chief of the shepherds whom Saul had'. But the word used here, *'abbîr*, is not used of position or status but always of strength; in human terms, of sheer physical toughness.

In an agricultural economy, of course, shepherds were important people, not least where significant estates were involved, as seems to have been the case with Saul (2 Samuel 9:7–10), and, among the shepherds, Doeg the outsider, the Edomite, had won his way – he was 'the mighty one',[1] the 'tough guy' in the shepherding community. Was it his readiness with his fists that got him into trouble and into jail? It's a likely enough scenario – and well matches the picture of unscrupulous, determined self-advancement that shines between the lines of Psalm 52:1–4.

Intersecting orbits

We might say what bad luck that Doeg, of all people, was there at Nob when David came to put a 'spin' of deception on his situation. But life is like that. People's orbits intersect. You never know who's seeing, who's listening. Nothing but unremitting straightforwardness and self-subordination to the other man's welfare will do. For David spotted Doeg, and his antennae quivered. He knew the man spelled trouble (1 Samuel 22:22). Why, then, did he persist in implicating Ahimelech in what could be construed as an anti-Saul conspiracy? Why did he not say in a loud voice, so that the eavesdropper must hear, 'Oh yes, of course I understand that you can't help me. You're quite right. Loyalty to His Majesty must come first! No food! No weapons!' – and then quietly take himself off? But no, he had been more than economical with the truth himself and now he must either eat humble pie and confess or leave events to fester. He chose the latter.

Meanwhile, back at Saul's ...

Saul's paranoia was now in full command of the poor, sad king. He felt every man's hand was against him; no one understood; and after all he had done for them, too (1 Samuel 22:6–8)! Doeg knew just how to 'spin' what he had seen at Nob. 'Economical with the truth' was his middle name! He told only how the priest had helped David, but said nothing about the rest of the story: how David had deceived and misled and lied to the priest. Furthermore, if Saul wanted vengeance on the priests, Doeg was his man. He wasn't the 'tough guy' for nothing – besides, he had had quite enough of priests and their ways while he was 'inside'.

So David lied, and Doeg lied. They used the truth to corrupt the truth – another definition of a 'white lie'. They used their tongues as instruments for their own advantage, and the whole priestly family was done to death.

Such is the power of the tongue to hurt and destroy.

David's diary

When we turn back, now, to Psalm 52, its suitability for the situation sketched in the title is plain. But, as we have seen, Doeg's tongue was not the only one at fault, and the obvious interpretation, that Doeg is the 'big fellow' (my translation) called to account in verse 1, is certainly not the only line to take, and may not even be the intended one. There is, without doubt, a reference to Doeg, but we must take seriously David's admission that from the start he knew he had set a dangerous train of events in motion, and that what he did was the 'real' cause of the sack of Nob. Without David's sins of speech even Doeg's practised tongue would have had nothing to spin and twist.

So who, now, is the 'mighty man' (verse 1), the 'big shot'? Even those of us who are at the furthest swing of the pendulum from Doeg, who are temperamentally incapable of his thuggery, who would not dream of taking up the sword in any cause or against anyone – and David was far from all that! – even we are quite capable of being 'thugs of the tongue', wangling ourselves out of difficulty by half-truths, gaining advantage for ourselves by disadvantage to real truthfulness. Psalm 52 denounces Doeg, but surely it addresses itself chiefly to David – and it comes as a warning and an instruction to us all.

So here (at last) is the psalm!

A¹ v. 1 Alternative lifestyles: self-confident boasting versus the unfailing love of the transcendent God.
In verse 1b the NIV (compare NRSV) opts to alter the Hebrew text, which says 'the unfailing love of the transcendent God (is there) all the day' (compare NKJV, ESV).² The Bible reveals Doeg as a man of arrogant and ruthless self-advancement. When David pursued personal advantage from Ahimelech by deception, he was buying into the same philosophy. Yet divine, sovereign undying love and care are always present and available.

B¹ vv. 2–4 Revelation! Behind the tongue lies a ruthless mind ('plots destruction') and an immoral ('love evil') and unfeeling ('love ... harmful') heart. What a person says reveals what a person is.

C v. 5 The exactness and completeness of divine judgment. Not 'surely God' (verse 5) but 'the transcendent God ('el) also', i.e., exactly as he has done, so 'also' God will do. The four verbs (see p. 52) are the measure of the Lord's detestation of sins of speech. This is the centre of the psalm.

B² vv. 6–7 Revelation! Time will tell. Divine judgment will fall and the ungodly mind revealed in ungodly speech (B¹) will be exposed to sorrowing ridicule – not malicious or sneering laughter but the laughter of wonderment that 'what went up like a rocket has come down like a stick', the laughter of relief that such an opponent is no more. Note how B¹ begins and B² ends on the note of 'destructiveness' – the same word is used in Hebrew each time. His confidence was not in what God could provide ('stronghold') but in earthly resource ('wealth') and dominant power ('destroying others'). 'Those who are right with God' (verse 6, 'the righteous') will be there to see it – and to learn the lesson. Had Doeg already 'come a cropper'? Or was David putting his faith on paper that it would yet be so? Whatever. Certainly he must himself have been busy learning the lesson, drawing the conclusion, as verses 8–9 show.

A² vv. 8–9 The chosen alternative. David commits himself to taking sides. The personal pronoun 'I' comes four times. His experience with Ahimelech and Doeg – and its tragic consequences – has proved to be a 'learning curve', resulting in his making a fresh personal commitment. So we have here (a) his prosperity and security (verse 8a). The evergreen olive[3] pictures constant vitality; 'flourishing/ luxuriant', abundance of life; planted 'in the house of God', acceptance and security of tenure. (b) His trustfulness and confidence (verses 8b–9a). 'Unfailing love' matches 'the unfailing love of God is for ever' (verse 1b), lost in the NIV, see above. Resting in that unfailing love was the alternative lifestyle to arrogant self-confidence. It is now David's chosen lifestyle. The voice with which he speaks is not the self-assured boasting of verse 1a, but simple 'trust'[4] and thankful 'praise' 'for what you have done', or, better, 'because you have taken action' (if Doeg has already had his comeuppance), or 'because you are certain to act'. (c) His expectation and affiliation (verse 9b). God's 'name' is shorthand for all that he has revealed about himself; 'hope' is 'confident, expectant, patient waiting'; 'saints' (hăsîdîm), those who have experienced the unfailing love (hesed) of the Lord. It is with them that David is determined to side, abandoning and rejecting his Doeg-like prevarication.

Notes

1 The word is *geber*. It is mainly used in the imprecise sense of 'person, fellow, chap, individual'. Occasionally it specifies the 'male' or 'adult male'. Again occasionally it has the meaning 'human being' (Job 22:2). Its parent verb is √*gābar*, 'to be strong, prevail', and this allows the ironic use (as here) for someone who thinks himself important or impregnable (Isaiah 22:17), i.e. a 'big shot'.

2 The Lord's *ḥesed* is the love he has pledged to us; love expressed in the will rather than felt in the heart. 'God' is here *'el*, i.e., God in his eternal and transcendent strength.

3 Is there a symbolism involved here? Noah's dove brought an olive twig (Genesis 8:11); olive oil was required for the perpetual lamps of the tabernacle (Exodus 27:20); in Jeremiah 11:16 the Lord calls his beloved a beautiful olive tree (compare Hosea 14:6). Note also 'house' (verse 8) contrasting with 'tent' (verse 5): ungodliness brings fragility, insecurity; to be right with God brings solid security.

4 In verse 8b 'for ever and ever' refers not to David's trust but to the Lord's unfailing love.

Psalm 54

7 A lesson well learned

Background reading: 1 Samuel 19; 21 – 23; 25

After his escape from Gath, David found a real measure of safety in the 'Cave of Adullam' (1 Samuel 22:1), where he also began to gather his private army. Adullam was in south Judah, and maybe David the Judahite felt he would find sanctuary among his own tribespeople. His experiences with the neighbouring towns of Keilah and Ziph (23:1–29) showed how wrong he was.

If David thought that running away from Saul would solve his problems, how very wrong he was! It was not only that the Lord could just as easily have protected him at court as anywhere else, but that moving from where God had placed him (and he had no divine directive to take flight) was the effective cause of all the subsequent woes for himself and, sadly, for many others. We might well see a parallel in the New Testament record of the Wise Men. Their 'calling' was to follow a star, but when they strayed from that path and, instead (logically), asked a king about the King, look at the trouble that followed![1]

Abiathar, a priest who survived the massacre at Nob, managed to escape to David, with the dire news of what had happened. 'All my fault,' said the distraught David, as indeed, from one point of view, it was. But the Lord has a way of bringing good even out of such an evil as Doeg's butchery, as we will see.

Keilah and Ziph: Oh, what a tangled web!

When Abiathar came to him, David was still a refugee in the Cave of Adullam in mid-southern Judah. By this time he had a private army, which had grown to six hundred men, all in one way or another disaffected under Saul's government. The town of Keilah was only a few miles south of Adullam, and Ziph, which also figures in this story, was maybe ten miles further south again. In other words, David, the Judahite, was well within his own tribal territory and, as indeed he may have thought, safe among his fellow tribespeople. Events were to prove him wrong. Rather, his dislocated relationship with Saul (which was not David's doing) was, as a result of David's flight, about to 'go public'; people were going to take sides; the personal divide was about to infect the nation.

The whole episode of Keilah and Ziph is actually much to David's credit. Had he consulted self-interest he would have remained hidden at Adullam, and left Keilah to take its chances with the Philistine marauders. If it was the Lord's choice to send him on this errand of mercy, it was David's choice to raise the matter with the Lord – even against the advice of his men. David had been made something of a national champion under Saul, but, over and above this, it would seem that the more Saul's kingship evaporated, the more David consciously cast himself into the role of king-in-waiting, as, indeed, was his right in the light of 1 Samuel 16:1–13. Naturally, therefore, he wanted to put things right for the people of Keilah when the loss of a whole harvest threatened them with starvation.

The ephod

It was surely not just some stroke of luck that Abiathar came equipped with the priestly ephod. It was the Lord's plan that David should have this means of divine guidance available to him. Out of

David's blameworthy behaviour at Nob there emerged this great good, for not even our meanest and most culpable acts can turn the Lord from his purposes of goodness and grace.

The ephod was part of the high-priestly attire and is described in Exodus 28:6–30. Strictly speaking, the name 'ephod' belongs to a sort of waistcoat the high priest wore on great ceremonial occasions, but 'the ephod' came to include two other items invariably linked to it: first, the 'breastpiece' a jewelled pouch fastened to the front of the ephod, and, second, the two rather mysterious objects kept in the pouch and themselves the means of divine guidance, the Urim and Thummim.[2]

When the Lord was 'enquired of' by this means he was addressed in questions requiring yes/no answers. There is no example of the Lord saying 'no', but 1 Samuel 28:6 shows that the Lord could refuse to answer. More than this we hardly know, but it is plausible that the Urim (meaning 'lights') and the Thummim (meaning 'perfections') had each a 'yes' and a 'no' side so that when the priest solemnly took each out of the 'breastpiece' two 'yeses' meant 'yes', two noes meant 'no', and a 'yes' and a 'no' meant no answer. Possibly . . . maybe . . . At any rate, this supernatural means of knowing the Lord's will was made available to David, and was part of the Lord's concerned and preserving love.

The even harsher blow at Ziph

David must have been savagely disappointed that his gratuitous intervention at Keilah met with such a non-appreciative (to say the least) response, but the Lord's reply gave him and his men time to scatter (1 Samuel 23:13) and then to regroup in the rugged terrain around Ziph, where he experienced another aspect of divine care: the Lord simply did not allow Saul to find him (verse 14). Matching the supernatural factor of guidance in verse 12, this is the sheer providence of God, secretly at work for the preservation of his elect.

Don't, however, blame the Ziphites when they simply took it upon themselves to inform against David. Saul was their king, appointed by the Lord, accepted by popular acclaim. He was very properly their first loyalty, and the action of the Ziphites shows what a loved king he was, and what a great leader he might have been. Yet their correct loyalty put David at potentially terminal risk. But the Lord had yet another weapon in his armoury of gracious and powerful care. He is Lord of all the earth, Lord and ruler of history. What are even the Philistines but a tool in his hands for David's protection (1 Samuel 23:27–28)?

The crunch moment

The history in 1 Samuel is, of course, full of the lessons of hindsight. We know therefore that, though David was often at risk, he was never in danger. The divine protective covering was always securely in place, and never fractured. But, for David, the future was rushing at him, with threat after threat and risk after risk, calling for quick reactions. For a resourceful, quick-acting person such as David, how easy it would have been to lash out at the people of Keilah. Maybe if they had been taught what a risky business it was to get on the wrong side of David, the Ziphites might have thought twice before sending their reports to Saul.

Maybe! But we can hardly be wrong in imagining three items from recent experience pointing David in a different direction: first, the memory of the consequences of his thoughtless, self-reliant lies to Ahimelech at Nob; second, how paths of escape opened when he sought the Lord's guidance at Keilah; and, third, the influence of Jonathan's visit, when his friend 'helped him to find strength in God' – and did so (1 Samuel 23:17) simply by reminding him of God's purpose and promise for him.

In Psalm 54 we join David at the very moment when he comes face to face with the extreme danger in which the Ziphites placed him, for when the local population became a network of informers there was no longer any hope that he could hide his whereabouts. At the heart of the psalm we learn how David saw the threat and how he faced it:

B¹ v. 3 God ignored
David's foes: who they are ('strangers'); what they are capable of ('ruthless'); how they behave ('without regard for God')

B^2 vv. 4–5 God upholding
David's confidence in divine help, sustaining, and
exact justice

David has indeed learned his lesson well. His hand has been strengthened in God. The fearsomeness of the opposition is more than matched by the God who is on his side. Let them do their worst; the outcome is not for a moment in doubt.

David's sense of alienation

There is a world of agony in the word 'strangers', for it was David's own countrymen who were hunting him – the Benjamites gathered round Saul – and his own fellow tribespeople, the Judahite people of Keilah and Ziph, who were the cause of his immediate crisis. Yet they were behaving as only foreigners would and could. Had things come to this pass that they could no longer see David as in any sense 'one of their own', deserving some sort of covenant fellow feeling at their hands? Apparently not! 'Ruthless' well catches the meaning and the feeling of 'ārîṣ, one who possesses superior strength and is prepared to use it with terrifying cruelty. If only they had sought God, and given him a controlling 'say', they would not be like that, but on this occasion, Israelites though they were, the gracious God of Israel was not a factor in their planning.

David's certainty in God: help and strength

But in fact there is no more pointless exercise than excluding God from a situation. 'Help' means that it is present and active; 'sustains' or 'upholds' means that in particular he imparts his strength and shares his vitality so as to make the unbearable bearable, so that David feels he is no longer dependent on such resilience as he might himself possess ('my life'), but is infused with divine life.

Divine justice

There are two possible ways of understanding the opening line of verse 5, with each expressing an important truth. 'Let evil recoil' or 'evil will recoil' reminds us that justice, moral recompense, is built into the way things work in God's world. He is God the Creator and his laws operate to uphold his moral and physical order. Over and over this is for our good: we learn, both by the teaching of our elders and by harsh experience, that fire will burn our fingers. If we insist on poking a finger into the fire, 'the wrath of God' – his providence working for our warning – makes sure the finger suffers. The same is true, for example, with sexually transmitted diseases. Experience teaches that promiscuity brings illness and even death; fidelity is the way of health. This again is a working of God's providential wrath – his 'warning shot across our bows'.

That is the way things are in the Creator's world. The price of being human is that we learn by trial and error and are responsible for the way we live under his providential arrangements. The verse, however, can be translated 'He will bring back evil on my enemies', that is to say, the moral rules of the world do not always operate in a blind, mechanical way, as does the law of the burnt finger. The Lord God remains in executive charge of his own rules. A lifelong chain smoker lives in robust health to a ripe old age, while a moderate smoker quickly contracts lung cancer. Life's like that, but it is not 'the way the cookie crumbles'; it is the decision of the totally wise, ever-just, unfailingly loving and all-powerful God.

Whatever way, we take verse 5a, then, David is content to leave the outcome of his trials to the decision of the highest possible court – 'the Judge of all the earth will do right'.[3] At the same time, his concluding prayer (verse 5b) makes his own position plain. His enemies are a mortal danger to him and he can see no solution except that they be destroyed.

This sort of prayer grates on our so-called sensitivities, but we need to beware of over-hasty, even unthinking condemnation. On the strictly human level, no one in a comfortable, unthreatened situation has the right to dictate reactions to a person in deadly danger. We must at least give David this credit, of being aware that no other solution would suffice. But, more importantly, since the Judge of all the earth *can* be guaranteed to do what is right, he can surely be relied on to uphold the honour of his own laws. In Deuteronomy 19:15–21 the Lord made it a rule for human courts that false accusers should be punished by themselves receiving what they had wished for the one they accused. Many if not all of the 'imprecations' in the Psalms arise from taking that rule seriously, and prayers such as Psalm 54:5b are the product not of savagery, certainly not of vindictiveness, but of realism. David could well have prayed (in a way we would find unexceptionable), 'Lord, please deal with them . . .'. But since the Lord will honour his own principles, 'dealing with them' will mean bringing upon them what they would unjustly do to David. In that case, the mild prayer 'deal with them' is simply evading the issue. They have made false accusations and demanded the death penalty; that is what will happen to them. They live in the Creator's just world.

May we, then, pray like that? May we actually ask explicitly for someone's death? Only if we can be sure that we stand where David stood! Firstly, that there is no other solution that we can see; secondly, that we have been the subjects of unjust accusation and that our conscience is 'as the noonday clear'; thirdly, that we can 'be angry and sin not' (compare Ephesians 4:26) – that the prayer does not reflect any vindictiveness in our hearts; and, fourthly, that we are content, like David, to leave everything to the Lord, taking no counteraction ourselves.[4]

Responding to the truth

The time has come to set out the shape of the whole of Psalm 54. At its heart David's overwhelming danger (verse 3) is matched by David's all-sufficient God (verses 4–5). The great truth that when we are helpless all may be left to the Lord has two 'outriders': on the one side, prayer (verses 1–2), and on the other, praise (verses 6–7).

    A^1 vv. 1–2 Prayer: the saving name

       B^1 v. 3 God ignored

       B^2 vv. 4–5 God all-sufficient

    A^2 vv. 6–7 Praise: the delivering name

Note how beautifully balanced the psalm is, with four verbs at the beginning – 'save ... vindicate ... hear ... listen' and four at the end – 'sacrifice ... praise ... delivered ... looked'. This, then, is what the psalm is still saying to us – both by what it says and by the way it is shaped. Intractable problems can be left entirely to the Lord. Our role is to pray (for the Lord ever works his wonders through the prayers of his people), and to praise (for the Lord loves to be thanked).

True to his name

The 'name' of the Lord is a concise summary of all that he has revealed about himself. The 'name' is the person as he is; the person is what his name says about him. Take the case of Nabal, the wealthy farmer for whose shepherds David provided protection, in expectation of a reward. None was forthcoming, for Nabal's servants had to admit that 'he is just like his name – his name is Fool, and folly goes with him' (1 Samuel 25:25). The man's name was a precise – if unflattering – summary of his character.

All the Lord's glory is in his name. Remember that a name and a title are two different things. The title (e.g. 'humankind') belongs to all in that class of being. The word 'god' is like that. But a name is personal, marking out the individual who possesses it. The title 'god' can be claimed by many, but there is only one 'Yahweh', the personal name of God the Holy Trinity. This divine name was known by his people from earliest times, but its meaning was not revealed until the time of Moses: we can read all about it in Exodus 3:12 – 4:17, but, in summary, 'Yahweh' is the God who saves his people and overthrows his enemies. That's it. So David is, so to speak, on to a winner when he prays, 'Save me by your name' – 'Act according to who your name says you are' ... 'Be and do for me now what your name says you are committed to being and doing.' How forceful, then, is the only actual mention of the name in this psalm (verse 6): 'your name, O Yahweh'!

Three verbs plus one

'Save ... vindicate ... deliver' are the verbs David uses about the action he needs the Lord to take. 'Save' expresses the idea of 'out of restriction, constriction, pressure into unrestricted movement', 'bringing into liberty', like walking in a broad, open land after being hemmed into a narrow defile. 'Deliver' looks rather at the hostile power from which someone has been rescued. 'Vindicate' is a legal word, calling to mind 'due process of law'. The Lord will never act wrongfully or contradict his own principles of justice and right-eousness. Here David calls the Lord in as counsel for the defence, someone who will rightfully win his case and gain the verdict for him.

We can include with these three great verbs the last line of the psalm. Like 'delivered', we can understand this as a past tense, indicating that prayer had already been answered. Equally, as is the way with Hebrew, the 'perfect' tense may be understood as describ-ing a future so certain that it can be said to have already happened. We would then translate 'he has determined to deliver me ... my eye will most certainly look...' This 'looking' is not to be understood as gloating, but rather as 'seeing the last of': David will survive; they will be gone. It is a vivid way of expressing confidence, under God, in the final outcome.

Put it into words; make spiritual headway

Two final things! Firstly, here, as so very often in the psalms, 'my prayer' is 'the words of my mouth' (verse 1). It goes without saying that the Lord has long since settled what he will do. He is God. He knows the end from the beginning.[5] Yet, at the same time, he does his wonderful works in answer to the prayers of his people, and he loves us to say exactly what we think we need.

Then there is the matter of praise. The order of events in verses 6–7 is important. There is something that comes even before praise itself: the 'freewill offering' which expresses fresh dedication to the Lord, a commitment to make spiritual progress, to go further and deeper in personal consecration, responding to him and to his saving mercies. Then comes the voice of 'praise'. But praise, too, calls for a proper order. True praise begins with God himself, praise for what his 'name' declares him to be, and only after that comes praise for what he has done.

God the Lord simply dominates David's autobiographical note on a particularly menacing episode of his life. In the Hebrew, 'God' is the first word of verses 1 and 2; it is towards the end of verse 3 and at the beginning of verse 4; and 'your name, O LORD' dominates verse 6. Yet again we come to a great, central Davidic (and biblical) truth. As 2 Corinthians 4:16–18 reminds us, it is when we sustain our concentration on the unseen realities of our faith that we can bear up under the inevitable afflictions of life. We need to learn, with Moses (Hebrews 11:27) to endure by 'seeing him who is invisible'.

David would agree. The only way to keep earthly things – including danger and trials – in their proper place and proportion is to keep *him* in full view, dominating everything.

Notes

1 Matthew 2:1–2, 16–18.
2 Compare Numbers 27:21.
3 Genesis 18:25.
4 Leviticus 19:18; Romans 12:19–21.
5 Isaiah 46:10.

Psalm 142
8 Into the darkness: man-forsaken, not God-forsaken

Background reading: 1 Samuel 19 – 22; 24

David, who had once known the comforts of a wealthy home, and then the (dubious) delights of Saul's court, is now a resident of a cave in south Judah!

David had at least two 'cave experiences', recorded in 1 Samuel 22:1 and 24:3, but actually, throughout that whole period, it was the caves of southern Judah that gave him the only home he possessed, and the only earthly security he enjoyed. The courtier had become a caveman.

From the royal court into the mountain cave – what a change! What an ebbing away of the good fortune he had enjoyed! What an unwelcome, unexpected and, to all intents and purposes, contradictory twist in his path! For surely the court was the 'proper' place for one destined to be king – to be on hand to mount the throne when Saul finally snapped? So human logic would lead us to think. But David's pathway – and the privilege of possessing his autobiographical psalms – ought to alert us to the foundational truth that ' "My thoughts are not your thoughts, neither are your ways my ways," declares the LORD'

(Isaiah 55:8). How I wish that we might learn this lesson – for every unexpected, unwanted, even seemingly meaningless, hurtful and destructive experience that takes us by surprise comes under the same heading. No, it is not pointless – it's just that we are not equipped to see the point; and, no, it is not 'the devil getting in on the act' and messing up God's good intentions. It is all part of a plan devised by a higher wisdom than we can ever know. 'He knows the way that I take' (Job 23:10) ... 'As for God, his way is perfect ... (and he) makes my way perfect' (Psalm 18:30, 32).

David's two 'cave psalms' – 57 and 142 – cannot be neatly linked with the two recorded cave experiences, though it is easier to link them with 1 Samuel 22 than with 1 Samuel 24. But this is unimportant. The important point is that the one-time darling of the nation knew what it was to be 'on the rocks' – very literally so – and both his experience and his thoughts about his experience are scriptures 'written to teach us' (Romans 15:4). These psalms belong to a very low time indeed in David's life – and they are in the Bible so that we may learn what the real truth is about *our* lowest times, and how we are to understand and handle them.[1]

Arriving: facing up to a grim reality

We must avoid trying to be too precise in relating Psalms 57 and 142 to each other and to datable moments in David's cave experience. Nevertheless, the feeling they convey is that Psalm 57 is a night-time meditation – maybe even David's first night in the cave's stony blackness, whereas Psalm 142 recalls the 'way' and 'path' he has walked (verse 3), hidden snares (verse 3) and his failure to find any refuge (verse 4). It can be seen as a portrayal, poetically expressed, of his flight from the court, when his home was kept under surveillance, when Samuel and Jonathan and then Ahimelech afforded friendship but no protection, and when Gath turned out to be only a further menace. The words 'way' and 'path' do not necessarily mean 'byways' but they can do so, and surely in keeping a distance between himself and Saul's secret police David would have avoided main roads. That he had a troop of men waiting for him by appointment was one of his lies to Ahimelech. There was no one, and by the time the cave, and possible sanctuary, came in sight, his isolation had plenty of time to grip his heart. All his 'halts' since leaving court – home to Michal, on to Samuel, back to Jonathan, to Nob and the priests, even to Philistine Gath – had involved other people. Now the mouth of a cave yawns, and beyond it the darkness. That's all; David is on his own – no wonder his spirit was fainting (verse 3) and his need seemed desperate (verse 6). If the cave implied safety, it also meant 'prison' (verse 7), for though pursuers might not get in, David can't get out! If not this cave, then another! This is now his life; things really have come to this.

And once again the thought rises, unbidden: would David not have been better to stick it out, in spite of all its threats, at the court of Saul than bring all this trouble on himself – and others? And if he now flees to the Lord for refuge (verse 5), could he not have equally have done so then? Trying to change our circumstances is a hazardous business. Wouldn't we do much better to acknowledge first of all that where we are is where the Lord has put us, and there we stay until he says 'Go'?

Reacting

Psalm 142 has three sections:

vv. 1–3a   Diminishing personal resources
vv. 3b–5   Isolation and opposition
vv. 6–7   Desperate need

Notably, each section ends by affirming a truth about God:

v. 3a   (better as past tense), 'It is you who knew my way.'
v. 5   'You are my refuge.'
v. 7   (literally) 'You will deal fully with me.'

Observe the tenses: 'You knew ... you are ... you will ... '

But the psalm is actually what it claims to be, 'an outpouring' (verse 2), and as such it is a delicate interweaving of three themes: prayer as the reaction to trouble; trouble faced and described; and the

Lord sufficient and triumphant. In other words, Psalm 142 is a prime example of what the Psalms as a whole are all about – 'Take it to the Lord in prayer.'

David at prayer

There are lovely and important lessons about prayer in this psalm, and the best thing is simply to list them as they appear.

(a) *Prayer personal, verbal, urgent, humble and frank.* All this in verses 1–2! 'Aloud' (NIV) poorly reflects the Hebrew 'with my voice' (see NKJV). Twice over David records that he put his prayer into his own words, and implies that the sound of his voice in the ears of God was an important thing – the Lord not only loves to hear what I want to say; he loves to hear me saying it. The verb used for 'cry' has the force of 'shriek', often with a note of terror, certainly with the feeling of imminent danger and urgency. By contrast with this implication of (so to speak) forcing ourselves on the Lord's attention, '(ask for) mercy' is, literally, 'seek the grace I need'. As throughout the Bible, 'grace' stresses the absence of merit or deserving on my part. Urgency must be balanced by humility, freedom of speech by recognition of unworthiness. 'Cry aloud' points to the felt need that drives David to pray; 'mercy' ('grace') describes the ground on which he prays, the undeserved favour of God. But we do enjoy the freedom to say just what comes into our heads, to speak to the Lord without solemn premeditation: this is implied by 'pour out'. Yet, balancing this, the verb 'tell' calls for a coherent presentation of how we are placed, like telling a story. Here, of course, is one of the mysteries of prayer: he knows it all without being told,[2] yet he commands us to ask! 'Complaint' and 'trouble' complement each other. The word *śîaḥ* means 'complaint' when the context suggests it to be appropriate, but its basic meaning is just 'concern', the inner element of somewhat anxious preoccupation; 'trouble' is the external circumstance giving rise to the concern. the Lord desires to know it as only we can tell it.

(b) *Prayer is the way to counter personal exhaustion of spirit, solitariness, misunderstanding, opposition and hopelessness* (verses 3–4). As we have seen, all these elements (appearing in turn in these

verses) ring true to David's situation. Taken together they add up
to a huge disincentive to pray! Prayer is a battle, not least against
our natural tendency, when under pressure, in trouble and spiritually taxed, to 'retire hurt', to get away alone into our corner, to
'chew the fat', to tell ourselves how awful things are, how unfair life
is, and how dreadful we feel. At such a time prayer is one of the
hardest efforts to make. 'Why did you not come with us to the Lord's
Table this morning?' asked a minister. 'Oh,' was the reply, 'I felt
too depressed to come.' That situation involved one of the Lord's
public, corporate means of grace – and in times of need should we
not fly to the means of grace? Prayer is one of his private means of
grace, and in verses 3 and 4 we meet David quietly telling the Lord all
about his situation. 'Spirit' is often used, as here, for energy, drive
and 'gusto'. But David found himself folding up under pressure.
'Within me' is the preposition 'al, regularly used to express 'to
my detriment, sorrow and loss'. Our own experience reminds us
what an effort it must have been for him to dig deep and find
the spiritual resolve to bring his exhaustion (verse 3a), his sense of
danger (verse 3b), his isolation (verse 4a), and his lack of support
and shelter (verse 4b) to the Lord. But he did. The reference to
his right hand is particularly touching (verse 4a). Just where a 'right-
hand man' should be, there is no one! But (as F. D. Kidner notes)[3]
the prayer was rapidly answered and the empty space filled, as family
and others came crowding to Adullam. Prayer was indeed the
solution.

(c) *Prayer is asking, expressing specific needs, and believingly anticip-
ating praise* (verses 6–7). 'Cry' repeats the verb used in verse 1, and
'say' returns to the need to put our prayers into words. The 'for'
in the second line of verse 6 is important. In verse 2 prayer was based
on the fact of divine grace; here prayer is based on the fact of
human need. I can pray to the Lord not only on the ground that
he is gracious, but also on the ground that I am helpless before
stronger forces and overpowering circumstances (verse 6b). Yet,
notwithstanding such hostile factors, the anticipation that the day of
praise will come (verse 7) reveals David's faith in the prayer-
answering God. With the Lord, even the worst calamity that can
come to his people never has the last word. Prayer will one day turn
to praise.

David recites the creed

(1) The past

We have already noted the three affirmations of belief around which Psalm 142 is built: 'You knew (verse 3) . . . You are (verse 5) . . . you will (verse 7)'. Look at them in turn. The Lord's 'knowledge' of our way is never a mere registering of facts. As in Psalm 1:6 (where the NIV translates the verb 'to know' as 'watches over'), his 'knowledge' of us is his superintendency of our lives, his active, directive, loving planning for us. 'Where was God', people ask, 'when such a tragedy happened?' 'Right there!' is the Bible's answer. He is a God near at hand, an ever-present God, close by in trouble (Psalm 46:1). There is a god (called Baal) who is never there when you need him (1 Kings 18:27). The God of the Bible, however, can be trusted as much with our misfortunes as with our joys; he is God as much in the green pastures as in the darkest valley (Psalm 23:2, 4). All our ways are 'paths of righteousness' (Psalm 23:3), that is, paths that make sense to him, paths along which his watchful love has directed our feet. When David said 'He knew', he intended to teach us of a God who can be trusted with and in life's miseries.

(2) The present

So much for his immediate past. David's creed included truth about God in the present (verse 5). As soon as he has lamented that 'I have no refuge' (verse 4), he corrects himself: 'You are my refuge' (verse 5). This is the God he described in Psalm 61 as lifting him above danger on to 'the rock that is higher' (Psalm 61:2), encircling him with the impregnable walls of a 'tower of strength' (verse 3), welcoming him into the protective hospitality of his 'tent', warm and comforting as a mother hen (verse 4). Even when he despaired of ever escaping from the unwelcome attentions of his foes, he knew he had a sure stronghold in his God.

As if that wasn't enough, there is also provision. The present tense of David's creed includes '(You are) my portion in the land of the living.' 'Portion' looks back to the allocation of the promised land to the incoming tribes of Israel. According to the rule stated in Numbers 26:54, each inheritance must match the size, therefore the needs, of the tribe concerned. 'Portion' in this way came to mean a sufficient provision for living. The Levites had no tribal inheritance but the Lord pledged himself to be their sufficiency.[4] All this lies in the background of David's credal affirmation that the Lord is his portion, that is to say, his security, tenure and sufficient provision. The words 'in the land of the living' are there to underline the fact that the Lord's presence and blessings are for the here and now – however much they may be transcended in the hereafter.

(3) The future

Like all good creeds, David's includes a clause about the future: it is a bit obscured in the NIV's translation, 'because of your goodness to me' (verse 7b), because the Hebrew actually has a verb here, not a noun: 'You will deal / act fully / work a complete work for me.'

In this third section of the psalm, David is still praying. The 'cry' (verse 6) is a loud, resounding shout because the situation demands urgency, and David would meet it with resolute boldness. David feels that his personal resources are spent (verse 6b), his pursuers have the upper hand (verse 6cd), and also the cave in which he seeks safety seems more like a prison (verse 7a). It is part of his praying to tell the Lord about his needs – a key lesson to learn, for if we talk about our needs to ourselves, we are only indulging in self-pity, but telling God is step one towards the solution. Consequently, as soon as David has spelled out his dreadful situation to the Lord, he immediately envisages the moment when the prison opens to freedom (verse 7a), when prayer becomes praise (verse 7b), when isolation is replaced by the fellowship of the 'righteous' (those who, like himself, are 'right with God'), and when, in answer to prayer, the Lord will put everything to rights, making a full requital, working a complete work.

Notes

1 Psalms 140 – 145, all ascribed to David, may be seen as a deliberate grouping. Only 142 has a title actually giving us its historical bearings, but 140 – 143 are equally suited by this period in David's life, dealing respectively with slander (140:3), provocation (141:4), loneliness (142:4), and nervous collapse (143:7). But in 144 morning dawns and leads to the great A–Z of praise that is Psalm 145.

2 Compare Matthew 6:8.

3 F. D. Kidner, *Psalms 73 – 150*, Tyndale Old Testament Commentary (IVP, 1975), p. 473.

4 Joshua 14:3–4; Deuteronomy 10:9.

Psalm 57

9 My darkness ... his wings

Background reading: 1 Samuel 22; 27; 30; Exodus 25

More of the same. Still in the caves ... still in divine shelter.

David endured a fairly long period of cave life – easier spoken of than endured, undoubtedly. The sense of aloneness, however, that pervades Psalms 142 and 57 suggests that they belong to his first days in the cave, before family and friends brought him companionship and also, humanly speaking, a measure of protection. As we have seen, this suits Psalm 142, where we share with David as he approaches the cave entrance and the blackness beyond it, and squares up to a bleak future.

First night

Psalm 57 suggests that he is about to spend his first night in the cave, with the realization that, with the coming day, 'the rest of life' is about to start. In verse 4, David prepares for bed, within the looming darkness of the cave and possibly with actual lions on the prowl within earshot outside. This is a very low point indeed – reflected in 'bowed down' (verse 6) – but, in a marvellously abrupt change of mood, David knows that he will awake to the new day with a new song on his lips and his harp at the ready (verses 7–8). The swing from being bowed down to being elated is abrupt. How could this be?

Psalm 57 explains all – and thereby teaches us its lesson.

A very structured psalm: verses and a chorus

Psalm 142 was an 'outpouring' – though it too had its broadly ordered structure – but Psalm 57 is much more meticulously planned. In the former psalm David captures his immediate reactions, without pausing to give them too formal a shape, but a few days spent by himself have seemingly allowed him to look back to that first bedtime and the morning that followed, and to put his thoughts into a well-considered shape.

Psalm 57:5 and 11 are identical. Think of them as the 'refrain' or 'chorus', following verses 1–4 and 6–10 as two 'verses' (or, in this case, groups of verses) – but, like all genuine 'choruses', they put their finger on the heart of the matter.

Please read the psalm using this outline:

A^1 v. 1 Prayer: overarching grace (NIV, 'mercy')
The prayer arises from ('for', v. 1) David's hurrying to God for refuge.

  B^1 vv. 2–3 Steady faith: 'I (will) cry/call out'

    C^1 v. 4 Enemies: their deadly threat[1]

      D v. 5 The totally exalted God

    C^2 v. 6 Enemies: their inevitable destruction

  B^2 vv. 7–8 Steady heart: 'I will sing'

A^2 vv. 9–10 Praise: overarching love and faithfulness
As the prayer in A^1 is 'explained' by 'for', so the praise (v. 9) is explained' by 'for' in verse 10.

    D v. 11 The totally exalted God.

First things first

When we sing a hymn or song with a repeated chorus, it is generally possible to see how the chorus arises from the theme developed in the verses. This is true of the final 'chorus' in 57:11. It gives expression to the central thought of verse 10; greatness of unfailing love is matched and supported by greatness of supreme exaltation. But when the words first come in verse 5 they are distinctly abrupt. David gives expression to a sudden 'mood swing' from dominant enemies (verse 4) to a dominant God.

That, surely, reflects what actually happened in his experience at that very moment. Suddenly his beating heart is stilled as the great truth dawns afresh that his God is sovereign over all, and that his glory (not Saul and his enmity and his prowlers) is the dominant reality of earthly life. Had he not always known this? Surely so. But in his moment of greatest need, and utmost vulnerability, it came to him with fresh power, as though it were a new truth learned for the first time. His foes most certainly are as savage and powerful and as determined to get their prey as hunting lionesses. But let them be as 'inflamed' (my version) as they will, with real power to hurt at close quarters ('spears') or at a distance ('arrows'), it all pales into its proper place and true proportions when the Sovereign God is taken into account – he who is higher even than the heavens themselves, and who is present in all his glory, dominating the whole earth – yes, even where the powerful enemies prowl; yes, even in the darkness of the cave; and, yes, even if David made a mistake in ever taking flight from Saul's court.

Step by step

Even if verse 5 marks an abrupt swing from verse 4, it actually fits well into the groundswell of the first half of the psalm.

Remember that in the Hebrew text of the Psalms the title is not a detached element, as the English translations make it, but is numbered as verse 1. Accordingly, then, the psalm begins with David literally 'in the cave'. But as he recalls that first night, and remembers looking up from his makeshift bed into the blackness of the cave's roof, what he actually saw was the outspread wings of God over-shadowing him. The rocks were real enough in all conscience, but there was a greater reality than the physical, a truer understanding of where he was, more to see than the naked eye could see – he was 'in the shadow of your wings' (verse 1).

The picture, and its underlying truth, is much, much more than a pleasing fancy. It is central to the Old Testament's thinking about the Lord – indeed, central to what he revealed about himself. To see this, all we need to do is go back to Exodus 25 – the making of the ark, the gold-covered chest containing the 'tables' of the law. The ark was kept in 'the Holy of Holies', the innermost shrine of the tabernacle, the place of the actual presence of God. It is even spoken of as the Lord's 'footstool' (Psalm 132:7–8), the point at which he 'touches down' among his people, and it was as the invisible God, enthroned above the ark, that he promised to speak through Moses to his people. But there's more! The lid, or covering, of the ark was very particularly designed. In the older English translations (AV, RV, compare NKJV) it was called 'the mercy-seat', a lovely, emotive rendering which goes back to William Tyndale, but 'atonement cover' (NIV) is more accurate even if less appealing. It was on this 'cover' that the blood was sprinkled on the Day of Atonement, signifying the Lord's acceptance of the sacrifice just offered. But – and this is the point essential for our purpose – the blood was sprinkled under the overshadowing wings of the golden cherubim.

Oh, how strong the wings!

David came to see this not only as a specific truth about his God in the matter of atonement – one who provides and accepts the effective-ness of subsititutionary sacrifice – but also as a true portrayal of his God, a God with wings outspread to shelter. And strong wings at that! The reference to the sheltering wings prompts David to cry out (call) 'to God Most High, to God who' (more exactly) 'undertakes completely for me'.

Abraham learned the description 'Most High' from Melchizedek, 'king of (Jeru)Salem … priest of God Most High,'[2] and, realizing that he was in the presence of a valid priest of the true God, at once took the title 'Most High' into his thinking, describing his own God as 'Yahweh, God Most High'. The new title means what it says: Yahweh is '(Creator, thus) Possessor of heaven and earth', the One who owns all that is, and therefore has it at his disposal, the Sovereign God.

'Wings' as such could seem a flimsy enough protection, but not if they are the wings of One who is truly and fully God, One whose habitat is the supreme height, 'far above all rule and authority, power and dominion, and every title that can be given, not only in the present age but also in the one to come', with 'all things under his feet' (Ephesians 1:20–22).

Nothing has changed; everything is different

Right to the end of this psalm David is still in the cave; the 'disaster' (verse 1) has not yet 'passed'; his enemies are still in 'hot pursuit' (verse 3), aflame with animosity. They are assured in their triumphalism (verse 4), and David is crushed down both by his distress and by the thought of the hidden pitfalls in his way (verse 6a). Yet suddenly the future is alight with hope and confidence. When the new day comes he will be there to greet its dawn with songs and music-making (verses 7–8). The prowling enemies (verses 3–4) will yet be replaced by listening peoples and nations (verse 9); the 'love' and 'faithfulness' that he expected (verse 3) will prove to be the dominant factors after all (verse 10). The sovereignty of God, affirmed as an article of faith in verse 5, will become the proved reality of verse 11.

Nothing has changed, but everything is different. Prayer has become praise; the shadows (verse 1) have become the light of a new day (verse 8); the roar of the lions (verse 4) has become the sweet sound of harp and lyre (verse 8). Prayer changes things; the Lord God changes things. Tell him all about it (verses 1–4); be assured that the emissaries of grace are on their way (verse 3); there is a moral destiny at work in the very nature of things which guarantees the downfall of evil (verse 6b). So be resolute (verse 7); stick it out; wait for the dawn.

This resolute waiting, however, is not a matter of gritted teeth and stoical stubbornness. In Acts 1, the church, which had been told to wait (verse 4), filled their waiting with prayer (verse 14). No one told them to do so; they somehow just knew that this was the right thing. And it was – and is. It is also what David did.

Knowing God

Coming to grips a little more closely with this most important lesson from Psalm 57, there are a few questions to be asked.

Firstly, would David have faced the grim realities of the present, and found such confidence for the future, without such a clear knowledge of God? Wasn't this – David's 'theology', his understanding of who and what his God is – the root of all his reactions to the blows life struck at him, the grounds of his strength in the face of such odds? His God was a God of grace (verse 1), power (verses 5, 11), love and faithfulness (verses 3, 10). Think about these things! 'Grace' (verse 1; NIV, 'mercy') is the sheer kindly goodness and beneficence of God, reaching out to those who have no merit whereby they could attract such goodness, or deserving whereby they could earn it. If David had not known his God to be a God of grace, would he have gone running to him for refuge with such alacrity (verse 1)? If David had not known his God to be a sovereign God, exalted above all things in heaven and earth, would he have faced the future with such glowing assurance (verse 9)?

Secondly, could he have entertained such confident hope if he did not know that the Lord keeps his promises? For David is looking forward not just to personal joys (verses 7b–8), but also to international fame and world significance (verse 9). Not yet has he been made aware of the endless rule and universal dominion the Lord has in mind for him (2 Samuel 7:1–16; Psalm 89:19–29), but he has been anointed for kingship – symbolically by oil, in reality by the Holy Spirit – and he is confident that the day will come when he will hold his royal place among the nations and peoples (verse 9). How then can Saul and his secret police have the last word? How then can the cave be all he has to look forward to? The Lord has promised! The word translated 'faithfulness' (verses 3, 10) is, basically, 'truth'. 'Faithfulness' is an acceptable translation, but in this sense, that when the Lord reveals his 'truth' he also binds himself to stand by it. His truth is one aspect of who and what he is, and, as Paul will yet say, he is the 'God who does not lie' (Titus 1:2), and 'he cannot deny himself' (NKJV, 2 Timothy 2:13). Peter slept calmly the night before his planned execution (Acts 12:6), surely not only because, for the Christian, there is no fear in death, but also because Jesus had spoken to him about what would happen 'when you are old' (John 21:18). Why worry about what Herod has planned, when Jesus has planned otherwise? 'The word of our God stands for ever' (Isaiah 40:8).

Thirdly, would David have been so earnest in 'crying out' to God (verse 2) if he were not sure that prayer is always answered? Not, of course, that prayer is a sort of slot machine where the coin goes in and the answer comes out. Actually, David's prayer was pretty immediately followed by a prolonged period of danger (e.g. 1 Samuel 23:26), by the (sinful) despair that made him slip over the border into Philistine country (1 Samuel 27:1), until he reached rock bottom – loss of home and family, and even of the loyalty of his men – sitting in the dust and ruins of Ziklag (1 Samuel 30:1–6). For, like everything else in this life, prayer is subject to that great rule of all rules, that ' "my thoughts are not your thoughts, neither are your ways my ways", declares the LORD' (Isaiah 55:8). Yet, as soon as David prayed, the answer was sent on its way, for we read in verses 2–3, 'I cry . . . he sends . . . ' The two verbs lie in parallel, the one 'co-ordinated' with the other: 'as I am crying . . . so he is sending'.[3] It's always like that!

Depend on it!

Depend on him!

Notes

1 A very 'jumpy' piece of Hebrew – as if we were listening to David's heart beating! 'My soul – amid – lionesses; I lie – people fired up – sons of man; their teeth – a spear – and arrows; and their tongue – a sword – sharp!'

2 Genesis 14:18–22.

3 Compare Daniel 9:23.

Psalm 18

10   Behind the scenes with God

Background reading: 1 Samuel 23 – 2 Samuel 5; Judges 4 – 5; Exodus 19 – 25

By 1 Samuel 27:1 David was weary of the caves of Judah and of running from Saul, and made a really desperate (and desperately wrong?) decision: he took himself into voluntary exile – to (of all places!) the court of Achish. Achish treated him with surprising kindness, giving him the town of Ziklag as a personal fiefdom (27:6). Meanwhile, Saul's reign was falling apart, as was the king's fragile personality. The next Philistine War brought both to an end, and first Judah (2 Samuel 2:4) and then Israel (5:1) invited David to be their king.

Who can read Psalm 18 and not be thrilled by it? Here is high poetry in the service of a divine rescue operation: prayer is heard (verse 6), and in response there are earthquakes (verse 7), heaven comes down to earth (verse 9), the Lord swoops down out of his clouds like some great raptor (verse 10), thunder fills the air (verse 13), the world itself is moved to its very foundations (verse 15), and David is snatched out of the life-threatening waters that were engulfing him (verse 16).

Great stuff – but when did all that happen?

Actually, it wasn't like that at all! When we read from 1 Samuel 23 (where David escaped from Keilah in the very nick of time, and from Saul by the skin of his teeth) through to 2 Samuel 5:5 (when at last he is king over the whole kingdom) – no earthquake, wind and fire! No snatching of David from flood waters! No storm or tempest, lightning, hailstones or coals of fire! Not a word!

Understated drama

In fact it was all quite different – exciting enough, but pretty low key by comparison.

David was saved, for example, by prompt decision, when he ordered his army to disperse, and committed himself to the uncertainties and vulnerability of flight (1 Samuel 23:13); again, he was saved by the ruggedness of the terrain (verse 26), and by the happy 'coincidence' of a Philistine invasion (verse 27). He was saved by his own sensitive conscience and Saul's fickle emotions, when, twice over, he refused to lift a finger against the Lord's anointed king (1 Samuel 24:4–6; 26:8–9), and Saul's fragile heart was momentarily won over (24:16–22; 26:21–25).

And next, David thought to save himself by the last-ditch expedient of self-imposed exile – indeed, so driven was he that he even took himself off to the court of Achish (1 Samuel 27:1–3), where, within very recent memory, he had succeeded in putting his head into a noose (28:18). How desperate and desolate David must have felt, not only to leave his own land but to cross into Philistia – of all places – and resort to – of all people – Achish!

It was, of course, as questionable a decision towards the end of his outlaw life as was leaving the court of Saul at the start. What had become of the David who could speak so confidently of divine deliverance, and of the certainty that his life was precious to the Lord? Sadly, in his lowest moments, David could not bring himself to believe his own most deeply cherished truths! But even so, worse was to follow. This time Achish must have thought he could use David to his advantage, and actually gave him ownership of the town of Ziklag.[1]

David, however, badly blotted his copybook by sixteen months of gross – indeed, grisly – duplicitous conduct (1 Samuel 27:7–12), and possibly we ought not to be surprised that it was in Ziklag that his career to date touched rock bottom. Dismissed by Achish from the Israelite War (1 Samuel 29), he returned to find Ziklag – the only home he knew – sacked, with wives, families and goods carried off by Amalekite raiders, so that even his devoted private army became so disaffected by loss that they began to plot his assassination (1 Samuel 30:1–6).

Yet in no time David was on the throne! Saul ended his blighted life, tragically, in suicide in the Battle of Mount Gilboa (1 Samuel 31:4). The news was brought to David (2 Samuel 1:1–16), and, directed by the Lord, he moved into southern Judah, to Hebron, and there the Judahites came and made him their king (2 Samuel 2:1–4). Just like that! Out of the ruins, on to the throne (compare Psalm 113:7–8).

Reading the signs

But still no thunder or 'fireworks', and the question therefore remains of what we are to make of the magnificent description of divine, literally earth-shaking, power in Psalm 18:7–15.

Judges 4 – 5 gives us a good starting point, because there, side by side, we have historical and poetical accounts of the same event, the victory of Barak and Deborah over Sisera. Judges 4:15 simply records that 'at Barak's advance, the Lord routed Sisera ... by the sword'; 5:20–21 offers another take on the situation: 'From the heavens the stars fought, from their courses they fought against Sisera. The river Kishon swept them away...' In other words, the same event has earthly and heavenly counterparts. On earth the battle has to be planned and forces assembled, swords at the ready, yet it is only the Lord who gives the victory, and to this cause he summons all the heavenly forces at his command – here, the stars – as well as the forces of nature – here, the river Kishon in flood.

So also it was as David looked back, recalling his hair's-breadth escapes, the 'fortuitous' incursion of the Philistines, his own force of arms against the Amalekites. The battle is the Lord's (2 Chronicles 20:15); he is always 'the commander of the army of the LORD' (Joshua 5:14), sovereignly apportioning the outcome. The standard Bible way of expressing this overmastering exercise of divine power is through pictures of storm and tempest, wind, rain, thunder, flood and fire.

Thus, in Psalm 18,

- verses 7–8: the earthquake, smoke and fire depict the Lord of Sinai (Exodus 19:16–18; Judges 5:4–5) still acting as of old;
- verses 9–10: the cherub speaks of the God of grace, the Lord resident at the heart of his people (Exodus 25:17–22), the God of atonement;
- verses 11–12: 'darkness' was the ninth plague (Exodus 10:22) visited on the Egyptians for refusing obedience to the Lord's word. Indeed, it marked the radical separation off of the Lord's people and signalled the ultimate judgment on their opponents (Exodus 10:21–29). The 'dark rain clouds' (more literally, 'darkness of waters, [with] clouds of mists') recall the great flood, the ease, majesty, and justice of the Lord's sovereign command of all the earth. The contrast of clouds and brightness looks back to the Exodus revelation of the pillar of cloud and fire (Exodus 13:21–22), particularly the Lord's presence as spelling ruin for his foes, safety for his people (Exodus 14:19–20).
- verse 13 should end, as, e.g., in the NKJV: 'hailstones and coals of fire', recapturing the frightening spectacle of hail mingled with fire of the seventh Egyptian plague. In Exodus 9:24, where we read 'lightning' in the NIV, the Hebrew speaks of 'fire self-kindling <"taking hold of itself"> in the middle of the hail ... '[2]

We see, then, what David is doing in these verses. His desire is to magnify the mighty power of the Lord, who is active and victorious on his behalf, and to do so in such a way that we too can feel the surge and pulse of the omnipotence that came swooping down from heaven (verses 9–10) to rescue him. In other words, he draws our attention to these mighty acts from the past so that we too may know that every awesomeness, every mightiness we see in the created world around us is but a reflection of the power of our God to save. What majesty of action! What omnipotence of intervention! What irresistible divine salvation! This God is our God for ever and ever (Psalm 48:14).

In tune with God's power

One of the great lessons to learn from the Bible is that it is much more serious to fall out of the power of God than it is to fall into the power of Satan. When we see in Psalm 18 just what the power of God is like, we realize that it must be so. No wonder David could describe the Lord as strength, fortress, rock, refuge, shield and horn of salvation (verse 2) when he knew that the Lord God of thunder, fire, storm and heavenly grace was ever active for him.

How was it, then, that this colossal outpouring of power came to David in his need? Can *we* learn anything about enjoying the power of God, about having him on our side in all his power, and about bringing his power effectively into our situations of need and helplessness?

We can indeed, and the first lesson is that power comes in answer to prayer. Look at verses 3–6.

A¹ v. 3 Simple prayer, sure salvation
The two verbs belong together: 'I call ... I am saved.'
In David's experience (as our study of Psalm 34 showed), this could be a pretty prompt saving answer to prayer in a particular need; but also (as David's whole career to date shows) the verbs can be taken as timeless, expressing an abiding truth – even, we might say, a law. This is the way our life with God works. Our sustained praying, his constant saving!

B vv. 4–5 The huge crisis
The danger to David was 'deadly' in the most real sense. 'Death' is not used here as a metaphor for extreme danger. He actually lived with a price on his head.

A² v. 6 Simple, urgent prayer, a sure hearing
'Distress' is countered by the simplicity of 'calling' to the Lord. The basic idea of 'distress' is 'in straits', being 'restricted, cramped', like what we call being 'under pressure'. 'My cry' at the end of the verse should be 'my cry for help', matching the verb two lines previously. It relates the general 'calling' directly to the felt need, making the prayer specific.

If we could have gone to David while he was under the enormous pressures described in verses 5–6 and said, 'What are you doing about it?', he would have replied, 'Oh, I am praying.' That's all! It was prayer that made the difference, and thoughtful reading of verses 4–6 and 7–15 should enable us to catch the vision of the almighty, encircling power waiting to be triggered by our simple 'calling'.

Walking in the way of blessing

When we turn to verses 20–45, on the other side of the 'fireworks' verses, we seem to find ourselves in a different world altogether, and, at first sight, one that is more than a bit off-putting. David, who seemed to be dealing with his problems by prayer (verses 3–6), now seems to be relying on his good works and good character (e.g. verses 20–24). Before we look at any details of these verses we must try to understand what David means by referring to his righteousness in this way.

Firstly, the wide-ranging claims in verses 20–24 must be interpreted within the setting the psalm proposes for itself in the heading. There is no way David is claiming a total holiness of life when he affirms righteousness and cleanness (verse 20), obedience (verses 21, 22), and blamelessness before God (verse 23). We know better! We have followed David through his miserable fugitive days from the start. It was more than probably a sinful lapse of faith that made him take flight in the first place, as if the Lord could not guard him at court just as easily as in a cave! Certainly he had no need to be economical with the truth to Ahimelech, culpably implicating the priests in his deceptions, and presently bringing about their death. And do you recall his behaviour in Gath? And the way he went on to pull the wool over Achish's eyes when that somewhat gullible ruler had been kind enough to give him a free hand in Ziklag? No, no, it would need an uncommon, pretty pathological, degree of self-deception for that David to claim sinlessness! But – and this is the point – within the narrower compass of his dealings with Saul he had indeed been righteous; his hands were more than clean in his relationships with the Lord's damaged anointed; here he had kept scrupulously to the Lord's way and word, even when his closest colleagues counselled otherwise.

Secondly, when David speaks of the Lord's 'rewarding' him for this righteousness, he is not suddenly turning to salvation by works. The idea of rewards runs through the whole Bible. The Lord Jesus taught that those who give even a drink of water will not lose their reward (Matthew 10:42), and he counselled the Philadelphians to grasp what they had so as not to lose their crown (Revelation 3:11). Peter affirmed that God gives his Holy Spirit to those who obey him (Acts 5:32). John calls for watchfulness so as not to lose what we have worked for, but rather to be fully rewarded (2 John 8), and in Hebrews 11:6 we read that 'anyone who comes (to God) must believe that he exists and that he rewards those who earnestly seek him'. Is this a strand of Bible truth to which we pay too little attention? We can put ourselves into the way of blessing, or we can rule ourselves out of blessing, and the key factor is obedience to God's word whereby we walk in the Lord's way and seek to live a life worthy of the Lord and to please him in every way (Colossians 1:10). It is in this way that we 'run in such a way as to get the prize' (1 Corinthians 9:24). It is in this way that we build in gold, silver and costly stones, in preparation for the judgment seat of Christ (1 Corinthians 3:11–15; 2 Corinthians 5:9–10). Paul strove to keep his conscience clear before God and man (Acts 24:16); so did David – and in relation to Saul he succeeded. He deliberately sought the way of blessing and he was blessed. This is the message of Psalm 18:20–45.

The plan and the themes

The verses fall into two pairs of two sections each. The first section in each case is about 'the Lord' and 'me' (David) (verses 20–24, 30–34); and the second section is about 'you' (the Lord) and 'me' (verses 25–29, 35–45). Each section has its own theme.

- Verses 20–24: the Lord, the Rewarder of righteousness. This is David's testimony, life as he has experienced it. Notice how 'righteousness' and 'cleanness of hands' (verses 20, 24) form a 'bracket' round the section and establish its theme; and at the heart of the section David claims (and, in the restricted context in which he makes the claim, does so rightly) steady loyalty and commitment: 'ways' (verse 21) are what we would call 'lifestyle'; 'laws' (verse 22), what the Lord has authoritatively declared to be right and good; 'before me' / 'in front of me', as the target I aim at; 'decrees', God's changeless edicts.

- Verses 25–29: the Lord's worldwide ways. What was true of David (verses 20–24) is also a universal principle, the way the Lord always works, rewarding all according to what they are and how they behave (verses 25–27) – including David (verses 28–29). In verse 26 'shrewd' means 'astute', always outmanoeuvring human cleverness or trickery.[3] Relate verse 28 to 1 Samuel 30. In the darkest personal hour, with the ruins of Ziklag all around him, his wives and children gone and his men turning against him, the Lord not only kept the lamp of faith burning in David's heart, prompting and enabling him to 'find strength in the Lord his God', but, astonishingly, turned the darkness itself into light by bringing him out of the sacked city, to Hebron, with family restored, men loyal again, and the throne at long last. In verse 29 'run against' could equally be 'run after', referring to David's speeding after the Amalekites. 'Scaling a wall' possibly looks back to his escape from Keilah.
- Verses 30–34: God's perfect ways. David always knew he was on his way to the throne, but it must often have seemed to him that his coronation procession was taking an odd route! But, writing Psalm 18, he is able to affirm not only that God's way is perfect (verse 30) but also that he 'makes my way perfect' (verse 32). All the twists and turns, all the hazards and deprivations – they were God's perfect way, and perfect for David. Nothing else would have been the best. Furthermore, God's perfect way is his servant's perfect training, developing the surefootedness that can reach the heights (verse 33),[4] and the strength that can engage in the Lord's warfare (verse 34).
- Verses 35–45: the Lord and his promises. This is the second 'you and me' passage, but, unlike the first (verses 25–29), which was almost all about the Lord's exact justice (verses 25–27), this is all about David. 'You' passages, describing the Lord's actions (35–36, 39–40a, 43ab) alternate with 'I/me' passages about David (37–38, 40b–42, 43c–45). It was claimed in verses 30–34 that the Lord whose way is perfect made David's way perfect. This is how he did it. (a) By personal preparation. The Lord

gave David salvation, upholding, greatness, and freedom[5] (verses 35–36), and consequently David dominates his opponents (verses 37–38), pursuing, persevering, dominating. (b) By giving victory. In advance of any contest, the Lord gave both the power to fight and the victory yet to be won (verses 39–41), and consequently David (verse 42) totally eliminated them. (c) By guaranteeing the future. Verses 43–45 make better sense if we see them as predicting the future world dominion of the Lord's king. Since the Lord will bring David to headship over the nations (verse 43ab), David will receive their subjection (verse 43c) and prompt submission (verses 44–45).

The gift and the battle

Look on the three parts of verses 35–45 as pointing broadly to David's present, past and future. In (a) he is the privileged possessor of salvation, which, from the moment it was given to him, remains as a shield of protection, and which brings with it the presence of the Lord, sustaining, promoting and stabilizing. David, of course, may have been thinking primarily of being saved from earthly opponents – hence NIV 'victory' – but we are permitted to see here the gift of our salvation in Christ, and to enjoy the related benefits of protection, progress and security. In (b) David looks back on many a tussle and many a victory, large and small – the whole story of his hazardous life to date. The Lord who gave him salvation (verse 35) also gave power for the conflict ahead, and worked on David's foes to immobilize them. Section (c) looks to the royal future and the fulfilment of the promise that David will rule the nations. We see in 2 Samuel 7:1 that David, soon enough after his accession, felt (wrongly, as it turned out, see 2 Samuel 8; 10) that his troubles with his enemies were already over and done with, so we need not find it strange that he had already been allowed to foresee something of the greater glory to come – of which the full reality is expressed in the later Psalm 89, and, e.g., in Isaiah 9:1–7. At this point the psalm becomes 'messianic' and (as we know) awaits 'great David's greater Son', and a future yet to be fully realized when Jesus comes again.

But while in (c) David foreshadows Jesus, in (a) and (b) he is our example. According to (a), those who are saved are a 'protected species', and walk a chosen, secure path. We happily identify with that, as indeed we should. We must learn, however, to identify also with the David of (b). The Lord's gift of victory (verses 39b–40a) is a call to arms. His victory is, for us, victory in the hard-won fight. His gift of salvation is a door into conflict. Certainly we have been blessed in the heavenly realms with every spiritual blessing. We already have all we shall ever need, for time and for eternity. But 'the heavenly realms' are where the 'powers of this dark world' and 'the spiritual forces of evil' operate; 'therefore put on the whole armour of God'.[6] Salvation is conscription, and we have a fight on our hands.

Adoration (verses 1–2) and praise (verses 46–50)

Every part of Psalm 18 speaks volumes to us. We read verses 3–19 and we are uplifted by a vision of the all-mastering power of the Lord who answers prayer and delivers; in verses 20–45 we find ourselves summoned to live the life that pleases him, in the sure knowledge that he with total sovereignty directs our lives for good, and never fails to keep his promises. Finally, the beginning and end of the psalm ask us, in turn, whether we do not long to love the Lord more fervently and praise him more wholeheartedly.

'I love you,' says David (verse 1), using here the word not of commitment or of solemn pledge but of passion: 'I love you with all my heart,' with emotions fully engaged. The implication of verses 1–2 is that such feelings of love for the Lord do not arise from trying to stir up our emotions but from experiencing the Lord, present, active and on our side in the realities of daily life. Look at the descriptive words: in weakness David proved the Lord to be the 'strength' he needed; in danger, the Lord was a place to hide, 'my rock',[7] a 'fortress' or place of strength in which to be secure. As 'deliverer' ($\sqrt{p\bar{a}lat}$) the Lord steps into some menacing situation to rescue. The 'God' who is 'my rock' is '$\bar{e}l$, the transcendent God of power, and here 'rock' is $tsur$, both the unchanging rock, reliable, always there, always the same, and also the smitten rock of Exodus 17:6, the active source of life. He is protective as a 'shield', as powerful to overpower as the horns of a mighty beast, and a true 'top-security' stronghold.

David 'loved the Lord' as he did because he had 'proved' the Lord's strength, saving and keeping power, reliability, faithfulness and almightiness. He loved the Lord because he had found by experience that the Lord first loved him.

All this leads us on to verses 46–50, where we find much of the same vocabulary but also a new and telling word. The note sounded is praise and thanks. David opens this section with the glad cry, 'The Lord lives!', thus summarizing all that he has said from verse 3 onwards. His career has been positive, personal proof of a God alive and active for his welfare. Hence, he goes on (literally), 'Blessed be [NIV, "Praise be to"] my Rock!' There would seem to be a subtle but important distinction between 'blessing' God[8] and 'praising' him. We can put it this way: when we ask God in our prayers to 'bless' some friend we are praying for, it is shorthand for 'Lord, please review their needs and respond to them', so when we 'bless' the Lord it is similarly shorthand for reviewing his glories, his attributes, all that he has shown himself to be, and responding in worship, reverence and love. To 'bless' God is to revel in what he is.

This, more than anything else, touches the heart of Psalm 18. David came to this climactic point of his life with a priceless knowledge of God, honed, tested and possessed because of the trials he had endured, the dangers he had experienced and the unwelcome turns events had taken. The Lord's way, after all, was perfect and he made David's way perfect.

Notes

1　Ziklag belonged to the Simeonite (Joshua 19:5) division of Judah (Joshua 15:31), further south than Ziph, but, at this juncture, it was under Philistine domination.

2　For hail as one of the Lord's conquering weapons, see Joshua 10:11.

3　F. D. Kidner, *Psalms 1 – 72*, Tyndale Old Testament Commentary (IVP, 1973), p. 94, offers the example of 'God's use of Laban to educate Jacob' (Genesis 29 – 31) and 'supremely by His unsettling treatment of the devious Balaam' (Numbers 22 – 24).

4　Compare Habakkuk 3:19. The Lord made David 'surefooted' in all the dangerous paths along which he brought him, until he attained the heights, the throne, destined to be his: 'my heights'.

5 Verse 36, i.e., as distinct from the hazards of a narrow path where walkers have to watch their step. On a broad path they can step out freely, without anxiety.

6 Ephesians 1:4; 6:12–13.

7 The Hebrew word is *sela'*, a 'cliff' or 'crag', maybe providing a cleft in which to hide, or a sheer height the enemy cannot scale.

8 The acclamation 'Blessed be the LORD' occurs about forty times in the Old Testament. The command to 'bless the LORD' occurs about twenty times, e.g. Psalm 103:1, 2, 22.

Psalm 30

11 Except the Lord build the house![1]

Background reading: 2 Samuel 2 – 3; 5 – 6; 1 Chronicles 11 – 12

David was as enthusiastic about being king as he was about everything he did. Some might even say it went to his head. Kings have armies; kings have concubines; kings have palaces. David will be up there with the leaders! So we meet him (2 Samuel 5:10–14) 'becoming great' in these stereotypical ways – and (even) Hiram of Tyre is rushing to help him to do so.

How long does it take to build a house? Those who have done it – or who have tried extending an existing house – will reply unanimously, 'Longer than we expected!' So it must have been, too, when Hiram of Tyre provided both the materials and the craftsmen to build a house for David. Hiram was moved to do this by his personal regard for David, but nevertheless it was also an indicator of David's international standing. Some of the 'glittering prizes' were beginning to come his way.

But how long did Hiram's men take to bring themselves and all their cedarwood from Tyre, over 100 miles away? And then how long did they take in actually building the house? In other words, the Bible can state the matter in one verse, but we may take it for granted that the work was still going on while David was engaged in the Philistine Wars, though it was probably completed in time for Michal to look out of her window and be embarrassed by the religious antics of her royal husband.

Michal and the new David

The Michal incident is of more than passing importance. We can put to one side the question of whether David was right to be so exuberant – and, Michal thought, indiscreet – in the way he expressed his praise of the Lord. We can reach our individual conclusions about that,[2] but can there be any difference of opinion that he treated Michal hastily, unfeelingly, even shabbily, and certainly arrogantly? He had loved her once – or, at the very least, been willing to respond to *her* love – and the way she had defied her father in assisting David to escape had put him heavily in her debt. Yet when he became king he was willing to use her as a political pawn in his negotiations with Abner – breaking up the apparently devoted marriage she had meanwhile contracted – only, finally, to consign her virtually to a comfortless house arrest in his harem. A new David! An arrogant and petulant spirit that brooked no criticism.

Not – in my opinion – David's finest hour, but pretty well of a piece with the different David that the experience of kingship was producing. For as we review the story of David we notice that up to 2 Samuel 1 – 4 David has faced the experiences of his life predominantly as a man of God. Like the rest of us, he was not wholly consistent. It was a serious lapse of faith when he fled from where the Lord had put him, and when, in defiance of all the evidence that the Lord was looking after him, he emigrated to Philistia. Nevertheless, 1 Samuel 24:8 and 26:9–11 are much more typical of David's ways. He did nothing to bring himself to kingship. He rested on the Lord's promises and awaited the Lord's time – and, in due course, went, in one great leap, from the ashes of Ziklag to the throne in Hebron.

Kings have armies; kings make war

So, then, having reached the throne of Judah, could David not simply have waited till the Lord gave him the rest of the kingdom? Indeed, *should* he not have done so, and should he not have considered Ishbosheth as 'the Lord's anointed' (as, of course, within the norms of the day, he was) just as he had considered Saul, and consequently treated him as a sacrosanct person? But no, kings have armies; kings make war, and instead of waiting for the throne, as the old David would have done, the new David promoted civil war between Judah and Israel, long, bloody and with dreadful consequences for the future when the division between Judah and Israel finally proved to be the fault line along which the whole nation cracked apart.[3]

Not everything, of course, that David did with his armies was equally questionable. Taking Jerusalem and making it the capital of the whole nation was a military and political masterstroke, and doubtless it was logical for the king to see to the fortification of his new capital – though the question must be asked whether, possibly, if David were making faith and not 'royal logic' his guiding principle, he should rather have taken into account (as Zechariah 2:5 later put it) that the Lord is quite capable of being a wall of fire around his city. But it is just as easy to be hypercritical of David as to be unthinkingly approving, and we must be careful. Nevertheless, did he have to copy the kings of the earth in collecting 'trophy wives' and multiplying concubines? Why did he so thoughtlessly 'do the Philistine thing' by transporting the ark on a cart instead of following the scriptural requirement of Levitical bearers (Exodus 25:14; Numbers 3:31; 4:15), which 2 Samuel 6:13 implies he knew very well? And why does 1 Chronicles include, prior to the bringing of the ark to Jerusalem, seventy-eight verses about David's 'mighty men'?[4] It could be – indeed it seems to be – that the royal David was superseding the believing David.

Both Samuel and Chronicles comment, in the middle of all this 'royalty', that (literally) 'David became increasingly great'. In his best moments, of course, David knew that it was all from God, and all for the sake of Israel, but Psalm 30 reveals another side: a near-death experience of sickness (verses 2–3), divine anger, weeping (verse 5), the pride that assumed permanent tenure, and the disaster of the hidden face of God (verse 6), the certainty of imminent death (verse 9), the dispelling of mourning and the replacement of sackcloth by gladness (verse 11). In his genuine spirituality, David planned the dedication of the house Hiram had provided for him, but the Lord stepped in with a firm 'Not yet'. Only the old David could be allowed to take up residence, not the new David all too conscious of his royal dignity! There was need of some sharp, corrective, divine discipline.

Presuming on divine favour

This is the background that makes the best sense of the psalm. We meet David in a mood of elated worship – literally, verse 1, 'I will raise you high ... because you have hauled me up' (the Hebrew term implies like a bucket out of a well) – and the psalm ends with the pledge of unending thanksgiving.[5] He needed this uplifting because some severe illness (verse 2) had virtually consigned him to Sheol;[6] he had teetered on the very edge of the pit (verse 3, implying the underworld).

What had brought him to this sad state, so that he was so conscious of the anger of God (verse 5), the hiding of the Lord's face from him (verse 7) and the terrors of a lost eternity (verse 9)? In a word, 'complacency' (verse 6)! 'When I felt secure' is, more literally, 'in my ease'. It is only the context that requires us to place a 'bad spin' on this word. As so often, F. D. Kidner[7] puts his finger on the pulse: 'easy circumstances and a careless outlook are seldom far apart'. So it was, apparently, with David, and we dare not sit in judgment for we too can so easily presume upon grace. Rather, we should learn to be on our guard, noting the points where David dropped his guard. It was this sin of presumption the Lord could not let pass. Beware, then! What is small and insignificant in our eyes may be colossal in his; what we leniently excuse, he can't pass over. The word of Jesus to the sneering Pharisees says it all: 'what is highly valued among men is detestable in God's sight' (Luke 16:15). It is all too simple to drift off course when circumstances become easy, when people praise, when success follows success, when, as the world says, 'the ball is at our feet', and then to fall into the trap Moses feared for his people: 'When you have eaten and are satisfied ... Be careful that you do not forget the LORD your God ... (and) say to yourself, "My power and the strength of my hands have provided this wealth for me." ' (Deuteronomy 8:10–17).

It seems, however, that David *did* forget, and it was purely out of mercy that the Lord did not abandon him to his pride in his own abilities, but rather visited him with an illness that threatened to be terminal, and which David rightly saw as due to the averted face of a thunderously displeased God. And what was it that displeased him? Firstly, the self-confidence that assumed security of tenure (verse 6). Secondly, the presumption that God's favour must continue (verse 7) to maintain him in strength. These are what the Lord hates: self-reliance and presumptuousness.

Not again! Oh, yes, once again! Prayer and transformation

Even that deadliest of all dangers – death without hope – can be solved by prayer, for, as always, the only way to flee *from* God is to flee *to* him! We must be careful not to let the frequency with which the Psalms teach this truth blunt our appreciation of the importance of what is being taught. In so many ways the single message of the Psalms as a whole is 'take it to the Lord in prayer'. The Psalms really believe that prayer changes things, solves problems, delivers beleaguered people, and brings whatever is needed. If the message is repeated it is because it needs to be repeated, and because we are slow to take it on board. So, then, this time round, let us make every effort to open our minds, hearts and wills to this great truth: prayer changes circumstances (verses 2–3): the 'cry for help' brought healing to the terminally ill David, and gave him life instead of death; the cry for mercy ('grace') and for a divine helper (verse 10) transformed David himself from wailing to dancing, joy and song (verses 11–12). Prayer made all the difference; prayer made everything different.

The high God, the lowly heart: thanksgiving and humility

The psalm opens with David's vow to 'raise you high' (verse 1; NIV, 'exalt') and ends with 'give you thanks'. These are, in their differing ways, the opposite and the antidote to the arrogant complacency and self-satisfaction (verses 6–7) that caused his downfall. The clearer our awareness of the high exaltation of our God, the greater our sense of our own lowliness; the more we practise thanksgiving, the more we realize that all is of God, and that every good and perfect gift comes from above. To see the Lord 'high and lifted up'[8] and constantly to acknowledge the bountiful hand of the divine giver guarantee a proper perspective on life – both in prosperity and in adversity (for there is always more to thank him for than to grumble about). Since David opens and closes his autobiographical psalm on these truths, would we be mistaken in thinking they are his main emphases?

Revealed truth: the guide to life

So much, then, for the way the psalm opens and closes: worship, prayer and thanksgiving. But notice the order of events within the psalm: the verses of experienced transformation (verses 8–11) are matched and preceded by the verses of revealed truth (verses 4–5). David does not say, 'In my experience darkness and threat were transient, therefore it will be like that for everyone.' No, he firstly affirms what is true about the Lord – that night is always followed by dawn, darkness by light and relief (verses 4–5) – and then tells us how it was so in his case (verses 8–11). Truth always comes first. We must not deduce truth from experience, but interpret experience in the light of truth. So when David cried out for help (verse 2) and his prayer was answered by healing and deliverance from his terminal illness (verse 3), he knew that this happened because his God was acting characteristically (verses 4–5) – that is to say, within the terms of his revealed character.

First, it is the Lord's nature to (if we may put it like this) 'tip the balance' in the direction of 'favour' and away from 'anger' (verse 5a). He is rightly angered; his anger is as just and holy as he himself is; but all the time – again, if we may put it this way – mercy is clamouring to triumph over justice (James 2:13). King Hezekiah found himself in just such a position as David had been before him. Isaiah diagnosed a terminal illness, but Hezekiah prayed and the Lord raised him up,[9] for, said King Hezekiah, 'the LORD was ready to save me' – or as we might put it (with only a mini-paraphrase), 'The LORD was all for saving me!' In other words, all the time, salvation not condemnation, favour not anger, deliverance not destruction, acceptance not rejection, are foremost in the Lord's own nature and in his attitude to his people.

- Verse 5a reveals a ratio between 'a moment' and 'a lifetime'. In other words, the Lord is 1 : 37,000,000 (at least) in favour of putting anger aside, remembering mercy, acting to save, receiving with favour.
- Verse 5b reveals a certainty. Comparatively speaking, anger is momentary and favour lifelong, but the dark watches of what the hymn calls 'the night of doubt and sorrow' can seem endless. Nevertheless, dawn has to come; it is a covenanted mercy, sure, certain and fixed, not by 'natural necessity' but by divine faithfulness. Habakkuk put it perfectly: 'Though it linger, wait for it' (2:3).

The introduction to this great truth provided by verse 4 is of crucial importance. First, it belongs to the Lord's 'holy name' to be and act as verse 5 describes. To love mercy, to be quick to pardon, to be 'all for' saving us is what he has revealed about himself. It is his 'name'. He is eternally what he showed himself to be in and at the exodus – the God who saves his people and overthrows his (and their) foes. Secondly, the truth expressed in verse 5 is something his 'saints' (verse 4) can claim as their own, and sing about. This is the way the Lord deals in everlasting love with those on whom that love is poured. Both his anger and our experience of his 'night-time' are expressions of his unfailing love.[10] He never fails to hear our prayer, or to spring to our aid. So let us in turn not fail in exalting him as he deserves, giving thanks to him as the loving giver of all, and singing the song (i.e. joyful response to a free salvation) of those who, without merit or contributory action, are the objects and recipients of the great salvation he has accomplished on our behalf.

Notes

1 The NIV translates the title 'For the dedication of the temple'. As far as the word is concerned this is allowable, for 'house' (compare AV, RV, NKJV) is often used of the Lord's house, the address at which he lives among his people (e.g. 2 Samuel 7:5). This translation, of course, makes Davidic authorship impossible; it means that the references to individual uplifting (verse 1), prayer (verse 2) deliverance from the pit (verse 3), from wrath (verse 5), etc., must be understood in a national sense; compare Psalm 129:1–3. As to what temple dedication is in mind, opinions differ: was it Solomon's (1 Kings 6 – 8), that of Ezra 3, or the (re)dedication of the temple in 165 BC? The view taken in the present study is that the psalm is by David, the 'house' being dedicated is that referred to in 2 Samuel 5:11, and – as will be explained – the personal references are to David himself.

2 See, e.g., D. R. Davis, *2 Samuel: Out of Every Adversity* (Christian Focus, 1999), pp. 67–69.

3 At the time of Absalom's rebellion, long years later, there were still fanatical Saul loyalists to gloat over David's misfortunes (2 Samuel 16:5–13), and the Sheba who later still called for a rising against David was, like Saul (1 Samuel 9:1–2), a Benjamite who found ready takers in 'all the men of Israel' (2 Samuel 20:1–2). To fail to heal the uneasy relationship between Judah and Israel – rather to promote it by his needless war – was a cardinal mistake of David's. The reference to 'gloating enemies' in verse 1 could apply to many points in David's career. Compare 2 Samuel 15:6; 19:40–43; 1 Kings 12:16–19.

4 1 Chronicles 11:10 – 12:40. The variations in the way Samuel and Chronicles record the history of David – the items included and not included, the varying order of events – are all part of the way history is properly written. That fine narrative historian Barbara Tuchman (*Practising History*, London, 1983) writes that the first duty of the historian is 'to distil ... assemble the information, make sense of it, select the essential, discard the irrelevant ... put the rest together' (p. 17); and, as regards chronology, she observes that sequence in time is not necessarily the best guide to how the story is told. 'Sometimes, to catch attention, the crucial event and the causative circumstance have to be reversed ... One must juggle with time' (p. 49). Georgina Battiscombe (*Shaftesbury*, Constable, 1988) thought Lord Ashley's years

at the Board of Health could be given the prominence due to them only by being 'treated as a separate entity apart from the chronological story of his life'. The Bible historians are true practitioners of the art of history writing.

5 The same verb, √*yādâ*, to give thanks, is 'translated' 'praise' in the NIV, verses 4 and 9, thus obscuring one of the psalm's keynotes.

6 Verse 3, NIV, 'grave'. But Sheol is not the grave. The body is consigned in death to the grave, but the spirit lives on in Sheol. Compare Genesis 37:35 (NIV, footnote); 2 Samuel 12:23. The testimony of the Old Testament is that the 'dead' are 'alive'. Since, however, spirit and body are separated, Sheol is, in that regard, a 'half-life'; compare Isaiah 14:9–12 (NIV, footnote). All alike live on in Sheol after death, but while, on the one hand, the Old Testament does not develop the understanding of 'hell' that is revealed by Jesus (e.g. Matthew 5:29; 10:28) and the New Testament (e.g. 2 Thessalonians 1:9), it does entertain a real hope of glory (e.g. Psalms 16:11; 49:14–15; 73:23–24). The 'dark' view of death in Psalm 30:8–9 is often taken to be typical of Old Testament thinking. This is a mistake. In Psalm 18:20–23 (see pp. 90–92 above), we recognized that David's claim to righteousness must be understood strictly within the context of the psalm. So here, Psalm 30 is not contemplating all deaths but the death of one who believes himself to be dying under the displeasure of God (30:7b). Psalm 30:9 accurately understands such a death as hopeless.

7 F. D. Kidner, *Psalms 1 – 72*, Tyndale Old Testament Commentary (IVP, 1973), p. 129.

8 Isaiah 52:13.

9 Note the same 'adverse' view of life after death as in Psalm 30 – and for the same reason: Hezekiah felt himself to be dying 'in sin'. See Isaiah 38:1–2 and 38:16–19, and Isaiah 38:20, NKJV.

10 Compare Hebrews 12:5–11.

Psalm 60

12 The Lord's banner unfurled

Background reading: 2 Samuel 8

My Bible (NKJV) introduces 2 Samuel 8 with the heading 'David's further conquests'. Sadly, we have to ask what business it was of David's to be making 'further conquests'. The Lord gave him his throne and kingdom without aggression on David's part. So why not leave all 'further conquests' to the Lord? Psalm 60 meditates on the mess David got himself into by being a stereotype king rather than the Lord's man.

The heading to Psalm 60 points us back to 2 Samuel 8, and together they form a far from pretty story. The three nations of 60:8, Moab, Edom and Philistia, figure in the history of David's wars as recorded in 2 Samuel 8 (verses 1, 12, 14); the reference in the heading to 'Aram Naharaim and Aram Zobah' is more fully spelled out in 2 Samuel 8:3–6, 12. Historically speaking, David was an unpleasantly aggressive neighbour – and one capable of horrific cruelty in victory and of pitiless slaughter in battle. If we read twice, as we do, that the Lord gave David his victories, we can only marvel at the sovereign mercy and forbearance that those statements reflect, and at the same time find ourselves unsurprised that such a man of war – indeed, a man of such war – was reckoned unfit to build the Lord's house of peace.[1]

It is very likely that 2 Samuel 8:1 refers back to the Philistine War recorded in chapter 5 – in which case it was a war thrust upon David by an inveterate aggressor. But what business was it of David's to strike (verse 2, NIV 'defeated') against Moab, and, as verse 2 implies, Ammon? In the days of Moses Moab and Ammon were protected people as the descendants of Lot.[2] Maybe the situation had changed since then. Maybe Psalm 60:8a points to a fresh word from the Lord regarding Moab, but even if it does it is no justification for aggression and annexation! The David who patiently waited for the Lord to bring him to the throne would have gone on waiting until his kingdom was extended by divine gift to its promised limits.

Dangerous role-playing

But, oh dear, no! David the king speedily learned to be a typical king, and, sadly, came to allow his rule to be directed by a sort of 'royal logic'. Since he was a king, surely he was called to act like a king. What is the point of kingship unless one has an army? And what is the point of an army unless one makes war?

There is no other way to understand David's behaviour in relation to 'Aram Naharaim and Aram Zobah'. Zobah lay to the north of Damascus, and, therefore, in relation to David and Jerusalem, was in the very far north indeed. Hadadezer of Zobah found himself obliged to mobilize to secure his northern defences along the Euphrates, and David, catching Hadadezer with his back turned, invaded from the south. Opportunity knocked indeed! What a priceless chance to extend his budding kingdom northwards.

Politically, of course, all these moves were astute. As we have seen, David had internal enemies and critics (Psalm 30:1), and what better way to reply to them than to show himself as a strong leader, to establish international repute for his new kingdom, and to turn potential attackers into tributaries? It is always easy to find things to criticize in a person such as David who wore his heart on his sleeve, but he was still the man after God's own heart,[3] the king who set a standard for all subsequent kings to aspire to, the chosen ancestor

of the Messiah, and as delightful and attractive a person as one would
ever wish to meet. Besides which, if he was at fault in playing out
the role of the king to the detriment of walking with God in patience
and trust, it was a failing in which we all find it tragically easy to
copy him – confusing activity with effectiveness, quick decisions
with leadership, making changes with making improvements; in a
word, valuing status above character and human opinion above
God's approval.

No, we must not sit in judgment on David but we must learn from
him, and from the Lord's sharp, life-threatening response to David's
royal blunder.

Outwitted – but with his wits about him

The opportunistic David discovered to his cost that he lived in a
world of opportunists who were, if anything, even better at political
opportunism than he was! Catching Hadadezer with his back turned,
David took his chance and led his army to the far north, where,
indeed, he achieved notable military success. But now David's own
back was turned! He had left his southern border undefended and
Edom invaded with such force and effectiveness that David, when the
news reached him, felt the ground slipping under his feet (Psalm 60:2).
The times had suddenly become 'desperate'[4] (verse 3), and David felt
as disorientated as a drunkard. David's kingdom seemed over before
it was properly started!

The end of the story was as dramatic as the beginning. Edom
represented a colossal threat (60:9), but in the face of it David
detached Joab along with unspecified contingents of his army, and
Edom was defeated in the battle of the Valley of Salt in southern
Judah. Decisive action saved the day – the runners who brought the
news of Edom's aggression to David, David's decision to leave
himself denuded of troops in a foreign and hostile land, Joab's
marvellous forced marches whereby the Edomites had advanced no
further than the Valley of Salt before they were confronted by the
armies of Judah, and brilliant generalship on the part of Abishai. But,
as Psalm 60 reveals, that was far from the whole story – even far from
the real story, the story *within* the story.

Understanding history

Psalm 60 is David's autobiographical meditation on the moment when news of Edom's incursion reached him and he found himself staring into a bottomless pit of terror and loss.

Defining the problem is always half the battle, and it is the measure of David's acute grasp of the true realities of his situation that he saw at once that Edom was not the problem, and Joab was not the solution. He had not fallen into the power of Edom; he had fallen out of the power of God. Edom was not his destruction; the anger of God was! His need was not to dispose of the threat but to get right with the Lord.

This is typical Old Testament thinking, and a lesson we badly need to learn. Our whole pattern of thought and our educational background seek to lock us into a pattern of discernible causes and predictable effects. We know what 'causes' rain, and we can make increasingly detailed weather forecasts – a simple illustration of the prevalent 'scientific' cast of mind. The Bible would not in the least resist this understanding of cause and effect, but would always turn our attention from 'how' to 'why'. Take, for example, Amos 4:7–8. The weather forecaster could 'explain' rainfall in the ancient world as easily as in the modern world. Things don't change. High and low pressures have always been around and act as they always have done. But, says Amos, this does not explain why one area gets rain and another does not. For 'why?' is a different question from 'how?', and brings into the equation a sovereign God who runs his world on moral principles of due reward and just retribution.[5] Or, to put it another way, there are causes, and there is The Cause, and there are two ways of telling the same story. One story – the lesser one – says that the world is governed by political opportunism, with each nation out for its own advantage and quick to seize its chances. Thus David exploited the opportunity offered to him on a plate when Hadadezer was preoccupied on the Euphrates, and Edom exploited the opportunity offered to it on a plate when David and his armies thrust north and left Judah's southern border exposed. The only secure course is to have forces large enough to guard against every eventuality and enough military hardware to outface any and every foe. In other words, to get involved in the constant leapfrogging of the arms race, and never go naked into the negotiating chamber!

But there is another and a better way. There is a sovereign God, a first cause, an almighty executive power. The world is governed by his moral decisions. There is no security except in being secure with him. The 'second cause' of David's calamity was the Edomite invasion; the 'first cause' was divine rejection (verse 1a); the 'second cause' was insufficient southern defences; the 'first cause' was the divine power that 'burst forth upon us/shattered our defences' (verse 1b); the 'second cause' was Edom's inveterate animosity towards Israel;[6] the 'first cause' was the Lord's 'anger' (verse 1c).

The problem cannot, therefore, be solved by 'working the system' – by mustering troops and arms and by generalship. These only tinker with second causes. Edom was not the problem; Joab was not the solution. Nothing can be settled until the issue between the Lord and his people is settled.

The banner of prayer

As ever in the Psalms (and in the Bible), the solution is prayer, first for restoration (verse 1b), then for salvation, help and deliverance (verse 5); that is to say, firstly, to be right with God, and only then for his transforming hand on circumstances. Nothing can be right until our relationship with him is right. 'Restore' is, in Hebrew, 'effect a bringing back for us'. We can no more of ourselves and at our own volition come back to God than we can bypass the cherubim that guard the entrance to the garden of Eden with the flaming sword. In this as in everything else we are dependent on sovereign mercy and divine salvation. Indeed, if we knew the whole story we would realize that even the prayer for restoration and the desire prompting it are wholly his gift to us. Salvation is always all of God.

See what power resides in prayer! We know ourselves to be alienated from God (verse 1, 'rejected'); his anger is such that he has broken down everything that might speak of safety ('burst'), verse 1, see above; the very fabric of our world is falling apart, and we no longer have stability or security (verse 2); times are 'desperate', and we don't know which way to turn (verse 3). Do we unfurl the banner of prayer (verse 4)?

There is, however, something else. Psalm 60 has a particular truth about prayer that is all its own. The calamity that overtook David was entirely his own fault. Even if his incursion northward could be excused, he was still at fault for overlooking enemies to the south. More likely, however, it was his gratuitous invasion of Hadadezer's land – a mere territory-grabbing exercise if ever there was one – that angered the Lord. If so, David was guilty with bells on. But, even so, prayer was the solution. In the Lord even the guilty find refuge; even those caught out by their own deliberate fault can fly to him for salvation and deliverance. For, remarkably, those to whom the banner of prayer is given are not only 'those who fear you' (verse 4) – that is understandable enough, for they are only too conscious of his holy alienation – but they are also 'those you love' (verse 5).[7] His love is truly everlasting – even – *especially?* – at the moment of his sharp indignation with us (see Hebrews 12:5–6).

Unchanging promises

There is an abruptness at the centre of Psalm 60 which takes the reader by surprise. It so obviously contrasts with the ordered progression governing the rest of the psalm.

A[1]   v. 1a Problem: divine rejection

  B[1]   v. 1b Prayer: restoration

A[2]   vv. 2–3 Problem: desperate circumstances

  B[2]   vv. 4–5 Prayer: salvation

A[3]   vv. 9–10 Problem: the God who has rejected is the only Helper

  B[3]   vv. 11–12 Prayer: aid and victory

Seen like this, the psalm is a supreme example of 'taking it to the Lord in prayer'! But the more clearly we see this pattern, the more urgently the question presses: how do verses 6–8 fit in? What are they about and why are they there?

Well, first, they are a word of the Lord: he has spoken 'from his sanctuary', a poetic and emotive summary of the Lord's promises about the land he intends for his people. They may be David's own compilation, or perhaps a word of the Lord brought to him at this juncture by a prophet who accompanied him on his northern adventure. In either case, at the very moment that threatens David with the loss of his kingdom, he is reminded that his kingdom does not rest on his abilities to win and hold it, nor is it to be lost by his follies, for the Lord has made promises which cannot fail.

The Lord's triumphant utterance covers:

- the occupation of the promised land (verse 6), 'parcelling' and 'measuring' it out to his people;
- every promised area: Succoth and Shechem represent the centre of the land, and lie, respectively, east and west of Jordan. Jacob 'built a place' at Succoth (Genesis 33:17), so that it was the first settlement to the east; he bought land at Shechem, and this was his first possession to the west. Chronology is reversed in the psalm so as to give pride of place to Shechem, which actually lay across the Jordan in the land of promise. Gilead and Manasseh (verse 7a) represent the northern area: Gilead in Transjordan, and Manasseh straddling the Jordan to the west and east. Ephraim and Judah (verse 7b) were the principal tribal areas west of Jordan. The reference to them goes beyond registering a claim to ownership ('parcel ... mine') to exercising ownership against all comers (the 'helmet' of the defending warrior) and setting up government (the 'sceptre' of the ruler);
- the overmastering of the nations (verse 8). There seems to be no biblical guidance to help us to interpret the use here of 'washbasin' and 'sandal',[8] and it is sufficient to think of Moab – for all its pride (Isaiah 16:6) – and Edom – for all its present threat – reduced to menial service.[9]

Thus God's word brings the Lord's promises to David's mind, carrying with them an assurance that the present crisis cannot have the last word. Edom may invade, and momentarily hold the upper hand, but Edom cannot ultimately win. The promises of God are inviolable, as Abram found when he tried to solve a domestic problem by dividing the land with Lot, and the Lord, in effect, replied, 'You can't do that, because it's *all* yours!'[10] So it was also with

David. In his desperate time – yes, desperate by his own fault! – the word of God brought the assurance he needed, provided a sure foundation for his prayers, and girded him for what was now to come. Is this what 1 Samuel 30:6 means when it says that, in a pretty comparable calamity, David 'found strength in the LORD his God'? In any case, it is the same for us: the Word of God, the holy Scripture, is our personal and domestic means of grace (just as the Lord's Supper and Christian fellowship are our public and corporate means of grace), and to them we should run for shelter, comfort, strength and direction whatever the need, wherever the fault lies – and, indeed, however deep our sense of depression and weakness.

The girding of the Word

Having been reminded of the promises of God, David seems able to look to the future. No amount of prayer, no soaking, however deep, in the Word of God, takes away the fact that Edom is still threatening the south of Judah. The enemy is still rampant, the kingdom still at risk. Yet at the same time everything is different.

The thought in verses 9–12 is in part compressed, but its main contentions are clear. Firstly (verse 9), David knows himself to be unequal to the task facing him. The strong city is *too* strong. Yet, secondly (verse 10a), nothing is too hard for the Lord. The negative question, 'Is it not you, God?', implies a positive truth. God is the great victor, even in the case of Edom! But there is a snag, for, thirdly (verse 10b), the God who is able is the very One who is alienated! The contrasting tenses of the verbs bring out the hopelessness, humanly speaking, of the situation: 'you ... rejected us, and you will not go out'. It is a statement of fact, not of experience. How can the God who rightly thrust his people aside now take their side? But wait! Fourthly, the cry of the helpless never fails to reach his ears (verse 11). The helpless Jacob, with his thigh out of joint and all the agonizing pain that brought, unable to stand without the support of the 'angel', spoke with the absurd boldness of the helpless: 'I will not let you go unless you bless me' (Genesis 32:26), and, says Hosea (12:3–4), 'he struggled with God – he struggled with the angel and prevailed!! He wept and supplicated for the grace he needed ... ' When he was weak, then he was strong[11] – the power of need, coupled with the power of prayer, prevails! Psalm 60 was David's moment of wrestling with the angel, and in his emptiness he discovered, fifthly (verse 12), that he could now say with confidence, 'With God we shall gain the victory'; he was, after all, back in the divine companionship; the Lord was, after all, on his side.

Notice, however, sixthly (verse 12), *who* is going to gain the victory. The whole psalm has been impregnated with the sovereignty of God. How remarkable, then, that after all '*we* shall gain the victory'. The force, under Joab's command, must hasten south; positions must be taken, plans laid, swords sharpened. There's a fight to be fought. The battle always is the Lord's,[12] but the Lord wins his battles on behalf of his dedicated, armed, committed, obedient and valiantly fighting people. It is to them he gives the victory. Three things belong together: prayer that leaves all to God, and looks for all from God; confident resting on the promises of God, expressed in his Word, which he will never change and never fail to keep; and the committed obedience of the Lord's army.

Notes

1 See 1 Kings 5:3; 1 Chronicles 22:8.

2 See Deuteronomy 2:9, 19; compare Genesis 19:30–38.

3 Acts 13:22.

4 Literally, 'a hard/harsh thing'. The NIV is a good emotive translation here, reflecting the reality of the situation.

5 Compare Deuteronomy 11:16–17; 28:2.

6 The personal tensions between Jacob and Esau/Edom (Genesis 25:29–34) developed into a national hatred. Amos, a millennium later, condemned Edom for an anger that 'raged continually ... unchecked' (Amos 1:11). The prophets, looking forward to the Lord's final showdown with the hostile world, used 'Edom' as a symbol of that undying opposition: in Isaiah 33:17–24 and Ezekiel 34:22–24, as in Amos 9:11–12, the downfall of 'Edom' and the coming of 'David', the promised, messianic, shepherd king, belong together. This looks back to 2 Samuel 8:13–14: David was the first and only king to conquer Edom. NIV: 'David became famous', literally, 'David made a name' – it became part of the Davidic 'identity'.

7 The word *yadiyd* expresses very tender, personal affection; compare
   the title to the wedding psalm, Psalm 45, NIV: 'a wedding song',
   literally, 'a song of loves'; i.e., the plural 'loves' signifies love in its
   perfection; 127:2 (the Lord depicted as a mother rocking her baby to
   sleep).

8 Taking off the sandal depicted renouncing a claim (Ruth 4:7–8);
   walking on land can be a sign of possession (Genesis 13:17;
   Deuteronomy 11:24–25; Joshua 1:3). Maybe throwing a sandal over
   Edom means domination and ownership.

9 The NIV adopts a slight alteration of the text about Philistia. As it
   stands it can be translated 'Over me, Philistia, shout in acclamation' –
   i.e., an acknowledgment of Yahweh's lordship. Moab lay to the east,
   Edom to the south, Philistia to the west. There is no reference to
   northern territories, which David was busy occupying.

10 Genesis 13:8; 13:14–15.

11 2 Corinthians 12:9–10.

12 1 Samuel 17:47; 2 Chronicles 20:15.

Psalm 51

13 The wonder of repentance

Background reading: 2 Samuel 9 – 13; 15 – 18; 19 – 21; 1 Kings 1 – 2

Even our best intentions can take wrong turnings. David's warm and loving heart is seen at its best in his care for Jonathan's son, Mephibosheth (2 Samuel 9), and, typically, he wanted to extend the same sort of fatherly support to the bereaved son of his friend Nahash of Ammon (10:1–2). His overtures were misrepresented and led to war. But once again David chose the role of the royal grandee, retiring to his palace and its comforts while his generals and troops took to the field (2 Samuel 11:1). Thereby hangs a shockingly sad tale and a complex web of failure.

Do you know the word 'trajectory'? A 'trajectory' is the curve made by a stone when it is thrown, or an arrow when it is shot. Leaving the hand or the bow, it rises for as long as the force behind it allows, then gradually falls until it reaches its target or hits the ground.

David's life, sadly, followed a 'trajectory', rising to a high point, then falling away. The high point was, unfortunately, not a summit of achievement. Rather, as the Bible tells his story, to a certain point David was 'on the up and up'. As we say today, he was upwardly mobile. After that point, he was on a descending curve.

The high point of the trajectory was his adultery with Bathsheba, and his criminal involvement in the death of her husband, Uriah.[1] It is all recorded in 2 Samuel 11 – 12. It is a grim reminder of how one thing can lead to another, how an unthinking lapse, followed by a 'quick fix', can have disastrous and prolonged consequences.

An unfortunate lesson learned?

2 Samuel 9 and 10 show David at his best, determined to 'show kindness', to live faithfully within covenanted loyalty. David had made a covenant with Jonathan, and he honoured it most beautifully in his care of Jonathan's disabled son, Mephibosheth. He also felt himself obligated to Nahash of Ammon for some unrecorded kindness that he had enjoyed,[2] probably during his wanderings. But this time – seemingly through no fault of his own – his kindness backfired. The Ammonites suspected him of having a hidden agenda, and acted with deliberate provocation, instigating a war that inflamed not only the area of Ammon itself but the Aramean kingdoms to the north, and even beyond the Euphrates. The result was a total victory for David's armies.

In the course of all this, however, David appears to have learned an unfortunate lesson: namely that, as king, he could spare himself the rigours of a military campaign, while still enjoying its glory! So we read that, in the face of the Ammonite-Aramean threat, 'David sent Joab out with the entire army', and took command himself only for the final battle. This seemed like a successful formula, well worth repeating, but thereby hung a sad tale.

With time on his hands, David took a leisurely look at the naked Bathsheba, abused his royal position, misused his personal charm, and made her pregnant. But, then – consternation! – what about her husband? The doggedly faithful Uriah could not be persuaded into actions that might have concealed the child's real paternity, and only the horrid expedient remained of making sure that he became a name on the casualty lists of the Ammonite war. It worked. So with Uriah safely packed away in a body bag, David did the honourable thing by Bathsheba.

Had he got away with it? Could he breathe easily again? No. Far from it. 'The thing David had done displeased the LORD.'[3]

The stone and the ripples

As a result of Nathan's ministry, David is led to repentance. But repentance is one thing; consequences are another. An act of sin is like throwing a stone into a pond: repentance is like fetching the stone out again, retrieving the situation; but throwing the stone in and fetching it out create ripples, which spread and spread. Repentance in itself does not stop them rippling and spreading. Such, of course, is the infinite mercy of the Lord that very often (most times?) he not only blots out our offence when we repent, but also stems the tide of consequences. He has promised to forgive his penitents.[4] This is his sovereign commitment, but it is a separate decision of sovereign wisdom to what extent the consequences of our acts are allowed to have their way, or are stopped in their tracks.

His sin with Bathsheba and Uriah turned the upwardly mobile David into the downwardly spiralling David. Things were never the same again. Firstly, his eldest son, Amnon, brought sexual deviancy right into David's family, and, since David was inhibited by his own behaviour from taking resolute action, Absalom took the law into his own hands and killed Amnon; David's grudging forgiveness of Absalom left an open sore, which became malignant, and Absalom fomented a nearly successful rebellion, exposing how fragile the unity and cohesiveness of the kingdom were. Next, an otherwise unknown Sheba rebelled, and David made some frightful errors in dealing with a Gibeonite complaint, until our final pictures of David are the toothless tiger of 1 Kings 1, at the mercy of conflicting factions within the palace, and the author of a scandalously vengeful – even cowardly and morally duplicitous – 'last will and testament' (1 Kings 2).

What a dire catalogue of decline and fall! Bathsheba had, apparently, been clever enough to secure a premarital covenant from the besotted David, but it was David's premarital sin with her that set his feet on the slippery slope. Yes, David was gold – and we must never forget it – but he was far from *pure* gold, and immeasurably far from the unspotted, unalloyed, super-fine gold required for the Messiah, and yet to shine with full lustre in his coming son.

An amazing moment

The heading to Psalm 51 does not simply point in a broad way to the Bathsheba incident. In fact it is concerned with Nathan before it even mentions Bathsheba. This is important. The psalm belongs specifically with 2 Samuel 12:1–15, and is, above all, a meditation on verses 13–14:

> Then David said to Nathan, 'I have sinned against the LORD.'
> Nathan replied, 'The LORD has taken away your sin. You are not
> going to die. But because by doing this you have made the enemies of
> the LORD show utter contempt, the son born to you will die.'

On the personal level, David is forgiven. Repentance brings immediate remission – both the burden ('taken away your sin') and the penalty ('you are not going to die') of sin are gone straight away. But on the public level, consequences must, in this case, follow: the Lord has been brought into contempt before those who oppose him, and there must be a public display of his hostility to sin and of his justice in dealing with it. Forgiveness is not favouritism.

So far these are truths that are applicable to every sinner. Repentance brings immediate remission, though the extent to which consequences are allowed to follow lies within the gracious sovereignty of the all-merciful God – and the older we get, the more we are aware that, for the most part, the just consequences of our sins have been stopped in their tracks, though we must not presume upon it. David, however, was also a public figure. Nathan began his ministry with this reminder: 'I anointed you king', and it still remains true that much is expected from those to whom much is given.[5] Those in the public eye are to be 'Exhibit A' of what it means to walk with God; because they are in the public eye, their private faults are public scandals; and because the people of God are one body their failings are doubly and trebly hazardous to the whole.

Behind the scenes: the heart of the penitent king

These truths, in all their comfort and with all their cautions, are, as we shall now see, what Psalm 51 is all about. It comes to us in three sections: verses 1–6 deal with the wonder of repentance; verses 7–15 develop this theme: what constitutes true repentance? What is the 'mind' of the true penitent? And verses 16–19 face the public consequences of the king's sin, and ponder the community of forgiven sinners.

(1) The wonder of repentance (verses 1–6): the Lord and the individual
Please read through these verses, noting (a) verses 1–2, prayer for a full pardon; (b) verses 3–4, the sufficiency of repentance; and (c) verses 5–6, the depth of need.

Great words
The psalm begins with nine great words in verses 1–2.

- There are three words defining the nature of sin: 'Sin' (verse 2b) points to the specific fault – be it of thought, word or deed; in David's case, adultery and accessory to murder, in our case, whatever we may mean from day to day as we say to God we are sorry for 'that'.[6] 'Iniquity' (verse 2a) means 'deviancy', pointing to the inner 'warp' in the human heart, the faulty spring that makes the clock go wrong, fallen human nature. 'Transgression' (verse 1b) is wilful, deliberate rebellion against a superior.
- There are three words describing the effects of sin: 'Blot out' (verse 1b, from the Hebrew 'to wipe' or 'to wipe away', e.g. tears in Isaiah 25:8 or in cleaning dirty crockery in 2 Kings 21:13), i.e. sin leaves a mark, which God can see and only he can wipe away. 'Wash away' is the launderer's verb, and points to a divine action that penetrates right down into the fibres of the sinful nature (Hebrews 9:14); 'Cleanse' is Hebrew $\sqrt{t\bar{a}h\bar{e}r}$, used almost as many times in Leviticus of the sacrifices and the ministry of the priests (forty-seven times) as in the rest of the Old Testament (fifty times), and views sin as a barrier between the sinner and the Lord, which only the Lord can remove.
- There are three words describing the nature of God: 'have mercy' (verse 1a) expresses the idea of 'grace'. The Lord shows an undeserved, unmerited favour, which the sinner may seek – all that the word 'grace' means throughout the Bible. 'Unfailing

love' and 'compassion' express the contrasting sides of the
Lord's love for us: on the one hand, the former is his
unchanging, solemn commitment, and on the other hand, the
latter is all the delightful emotion of 'being in love'. He will
never ever stop loving us, nor will his love ever be other than
an all-consuming passion.

How simple . . . how deep!
It is because God is what he is that repentance can be what it is. Were
he like the gods of earth, who demand their pound of flesh, we would
spend our lives and exhaust ourselves in all manner of efforts to please
him and get into his good books. But he is the unique Lord God of
Psalm 51:1–2, the Lord of grace, committed to us in unchanging,
passionate love. Therefore we can rest with him as penitent sinners.
This is what verses 3–6 are about.

- Verse 3. Repentance, verse 3a, is a candid acknowledgment
  and an ongoing awareness of sin. To 'know' is, here, to
  'acknowledge', to come to the point at which all concealment
  and self-excusing are past, to admit sin, to call this horrid spade
  a spade.[7] But (verse 3b) repentance is not a flash in the pan. It is
  a lifelong and deliberately sustained consciousness of our sinful
  status and condition. Such is divine grace that the Lord does
  not remember our sin,[8] but it is evidence of the genuineness of
  our repentance that we never forget.
- Verse 4a. Repentance affirms what the 'real' offence is. When
  David was brought to realization of his sin, he blurted out,
  'I have sinned against the LORD', and we want to interject,
  'That's all very well. But what about your mistreatment of
  Bathsheba? What about your complicity in murder? What
  about poor old Uriah?' There is a useful distinction in
  terminology between 'sin' and 'crime' – that we 'sin' against
  the Lord, and commit 'crimes' against people. David, by this
  reckoning, was a criminal (in a big way) as well as a sinner!
  With all this, the Bible is in agreement. The ordinance of the
  'guilt-offering' in Leviticus 6:1–7 is typical. Where a 'crime' is
  involved – that is, some wrong done to another person –
  ample restitution must be made, yet, at the same time, an

atonement offering to the Lord is required. In other words,
the Bible recognizes 'crime', but insists that it is also 'sin'.
Wronging another person is, at base, flouting the law of God.
David's cry of repentance shows that he was aware of this, of
the need to get right with God. In the matter of sin, just as we
saw above regarding cause and effect, the Bible teaches us to
go straight to the top.

- Verse 4b. Repentance has its place in the purposes of God.
  If David had not sinned and been brought to repentance he
  would not have a true sense of how right and just God is. The
  Lord had pronounced adultery and murder wrong, and passed
  his judicial sentence on them.[9] It is to these facts that lines 3
  and 4 refer: God has spoken; the Judge has passed sentence. But
  suppose David had got away with it? He would have prevailed
  against the word of God, and triumphed over the character of
  God. He did not, however, succeed. 'The thing David had done
  displeased the LORD', and David had, with shame, to
  acknowledge how right and just the Lord is. In this way sin and
  repentance bring the sinner to a truer appreciation of the
  holiness of God, and are, in fact, used by the Lord to that end.
  He does not cause our sin, nor is he implicated in it; but he,
  who is over all, through all, and in all (see Ephesians 4:6) uses
  even our sinfulness purposefully,[10] to confirm to us who and
  what he is, that he stands by his word, and will not lower the
  standards of his holiness.

- Verses 5–6. Repentance and the depth of our sinfulness. The
  NIV offers a very careful translation of verse 5. In the birth
  process itself, and, before it, at the very moment of conception,
  there was an 'I', a person[11] yet to be called David, and that
  person shared in fallen, sinful (referring to both actual and
  potential sin) human nature. The repeated 'surely' ('Behold!',
  or 'Look at this!') nails verses 5 and 6 together. Human nature
  itself falls short of the Lord's will and pleasure, but, at the same
  time, in its hidden depths, it is subject to the infusing of divine
  wisdom. It is to this hidden work in the depths of our nature
  that Jesus refers in John 6:44–45 when he speaks of the teaching
  and learning by which the Father draws us to the Son, and
  without which we lack all ability to come to him. Paul teaches

the same truth when he speaks of God's inner working by which we are enabled not only to 'act according to his good purpose' (Philippians 2:13), but, behind the act, 'to will' to do so. David was well aware of this aspect of the grace of God, and repented before God not only of what he had done but of what he was.

(2) Making repentance deep and true (verses 7–15)

A little reminder is appropriate here, before we launch further into this wonderful psalm. Remember that the Hebrew poets did not write what we call 'narrative poetry' – poetry telling the story of some event. Consequently, we look in vain in Psalm 51 for any description of the David-Nathan-Bathsheba incident. We would not even expect to find it! Like all the psalms linked with David's life, Psalm 51 probes behind the scenes. It does not describe events but considers them. We join David, then, as he ponders the repentance that brought him forgiveness even of such appalling sins, and, in verses 7–15, he is in principle saying that if repentance is as wonderful as verses 1–6 claim, how important it is to get it right, to shun what is superficial and go for the real thing.

Read through these verses, then, noting what they emphasize. As with all the parts of Psalm 51, there are three sections. In verses 7–9, the stress is on being acceptable to God – being made clean (verse 7), the end of the Lord's hostility (verse 8), sin banished from his sight (verse 9); in verses 10–12, David prays to become a new person, pure and persevering (verse 10), sharing God's vitality (verse 11), and enjoying his salvation with enthusiasm (verse 12); and in verses 13–15 his eyes turn outwards, to teach others effectively (verse 13), to have a singing tongue (verse 14) and opened lips (verse 15).

Look a little more fully at each of these sections.

Repentance is longing to be right with God (verses 7–9)

In English we have verbs such as 'decontaminate' and 'delouse', but we do not say 'de-sin', Yet that is the nearest we can get to David's verb ('cleanse') in verse 7, which in Hebrew suggests not just the removal of the stain of this or that sin, but the clearing out of every last trace of sin itself. Only the Lord can do this, and it is for divine action that David prays.

The reference to 'hyssop' (verse 7) is telling.

- In Exodus 12:22 hyssop was used to apply the blood of the Passover lamb to the door frame of the house in which the family would shelter. This blood made 'propitiation' – the satisfying of divine judgment. In Exodus 12:12–13 the Lord entered Egypt in wrath, saw the blood, and passed over in peace. He was 'propitiated'.
- In Leviticus 14:6 hyssop was used to sprinkle blood on the leper who was to be cleansed.
- In Numbers 19 hyssop is mentioned twice. In verse 6 it is one of the ingredients of the 'water of cleansing . . . for purification from sin'. Each ingredient in verse 6 is meant to tell us something about this water, and the inclusion of hyssop teaches that it is meant for actual application – as is described in verse 18 – purging away even the contagion of death itself.

All this lies behind David's cry, 'De-sin me with hyssop.' In his case, the law of the Lord made no provision for the sins of adultery and murder, each of which attracted capital punishment (e.g. in Leviticus 21:10; Deuteronomy 22:22; Genesis 9:6; Exodus 21:12–14). No sacrifice was authorized; no way of pardon and cleansing was made known. But David is confident – a confidence arising from the prompt word of pardon in 2 Samuel 12:13 – that there is, somewhere, somehow, a sacrifice known to the Lord, a sprinkling he can make which, even in this case, will satisfy the wrath of a sin-hating God, and purge the defilement of the sinner.

Restoration (verses 8–9)
In verse 7 sin is an uncleanness infecting the sinner, and repentance proves its genuineness by longing to be clean. In verse 8 sin brings the sinner into danger of divine hostility and personal destruction; and in verse 9 there is the dreadful reality of being 'God-forsaken'. True repentance longs for deliverance from wrath and for restoration to favour.[12] The dire seriousness of sin is its offensiveness to and offence against God. But to the praise of divine grace – as revealed in verses 1–2 – repentance can put even this right, and genuine repentance makes this the first of its desires. David could well have been thinking

in the first place of other things – the good name he had forfeited, the
damage to his royal pride, his family and his kingdom. These all have
their place in the total scheme of things, but way before all these
comes the Lord, his broken law, and his offended holiness.[13]

Repentance is longing to be a new person (verses 10–12)
New Testament believers are sometimes troubled by a supposed
contradiction between 'take not your Holy Spirit from me' (verse 11),
and the promise of Jesus that he, the Holy Spirit, will be 'with you for
ever'.[14] We need, however, to remember that the New Testament
itself warns us against resisting and grieving the Holy Spirit, and
against 'putting out the Spirit's fire' / 'quenching the Spirit'.[15] None of
these involve the loss of the Holy Spirit's indwelling, but they do
involve, while they persist, loss of enjoyment of the benefits of his
presence. Since verse 10 prays for a renewed steadfastness, and verse
12 for the joy of salvation, we may take it that, in verse 11, David fears
the loss of the benefits and blessings that God's Spirit brings. Very
possibly he is bringing to mind the tragedy of Saul, and dreads what
bad results his sin may bring upon himself.[16] Behind these verses lies a
solemn awareness of the frightful seriousness of sin, and a terror of
the consequences that it must bring, if left to itself. But the God of all
grace always has better things in mind for us, and we see these as we
join David in the perceptive prayer of verses 10–12.

He begins by desiring a creative act of God. Aware as he is of the
depth both of his sinfulness (verse 5) and of the humanly unattainable
standards of the Lord (verse 6), he flies in prayer to the only power
able to make the needed transformations – purity of heart (verse 10a)
and consistency of life (verse 10b). 'Pure' derives from the verb
translated 'cleanse' in verse 2, meaning a heart from which everything
barring or marring his relationship with God has been removed.
'Spirit' includes everything included in the 'get up and go' aspect of
our nature – our wills, our energies, our enthusiasms, our ambitions,
and our zest for life. If only all this could be consistently out for
God and his truth, governed by his Word, obedient to his law, intent
on his standards, holy as he is holy! If only we could be consistent! For
this David prays –and sets us a true example. The reference to a
'willing spirit' in verse 12 very likely continues the same thought, but
could it be, instead, a reference to the willingness of the Holy Spirit to

leap to our aid? Why not? This is a great and needed truth, and, in the Bible, a very lovely promise.[17] There is, however, no reason why in this case we should not have our cake and eat it. When something the Bible says is capable of two equally valid interpretations, the Bible writers, knowing far more Hebrew and Greek than we do, would have been well aware of the nuances of their own languages. If, for their part, they were willing to allow two possible meanings to stand, we can do the same. On the one hand, then, the Holy Spirit is the willing agent, alert and ready to lead us back from our 'far country' into the joys of salvation, and to be our sustaining strength as we resume the task of consistent living. On the other hand (compare Philippians 2:13), he can create in us and summon us to a new and fresh willingness to live for God, in truth, and with holy resolve.

Repentance is a commitment to sharing the Good News (verses 13–15)
The Hebrew expresses no 'Then' in verse 13. Rather, it continues the prayer-emphasis of the preceding verses – 'Oh let me teach . . .' coupled here with a personal desire and commitment to do so: I would undertake to teach . . .' The same voice that asked for restoration to God (verses 7–9) and to joy (verses 10–12) asks for restoration to service,[18] to the work of teaching others (verse 13) and to testimony to the 'excellencies' of God (verse 15).[19]

Each of the three verses shares an important truth.

- Verse 13 insists that conversions are the product of teaching. 'Transgressors' (as in verse 1) are those in willing and wilful rebellion against the word and will of God; 'Sinners' (compare verse 2) have specific faults and failings of thought, word and deed, in their experience and record – in other words, David looks around him at typical humans in all their spiritual need. Left to themselves they are helpless and hopeless, but God's powerful truth will bring them back from their disastrous ways. He allows no room for doubt on this point. Teach the truth, and they will turn back.

- Verse 14 adds this practical and most important observation, that effective, saving testimony comes from the tongue of one who is himself a guilty but saved sinner. This is the point of verse 14. David's gaze is turned outward to others in both verse

13 and verse 15, so why does he suddenly become self-absorbed in verse 14? There is a very good reason: do we not often think, 'Who am I to teach others?' Do we not often hesitate to give our testimony lest someone say (all too fairly), 'Who are *you* to talk?' David helps us over this hurdle. He puts a reply into our mouth – not a snide or evasive answer but a sincere and truthful one: 'Yes, indeed! Who *am* I to talk? But isn't that exactly what I am trying to tell you? He bothers with sinners. It is people like me and you he sets himself to save!' In other words, the teaching that is effective, the testimony that impresses, comes from a sinner saved by grace, the guilty telling the guilty of a God who pardons guilt and 'welcomes sinners and eats with them'.[20]

(3) The community of penitents (verses 16–19)

Balancing the individual penitent sinner of verses 1–6, and having explained the nature of true repentance (verses 7–15), the psalm ends with a whole body of saved sinners – with Zion, prosperous and secure, its life centred on 'righteous sacrifices' in which the Lord delights.[21]

There is an opening 'for' in verse 16 which the NIV omits (compare NKJV). David has been affirming his determination to testify to others what he has learned about the Lord. If the Lord will only open his lips, he will engage in public praise. The heart of David's testimony is, then, that 'I will teach' (verse 13) ' . . . because you do not delight . . . ' (verse 16). A God of mere (and hugely demanding) ritual requirement is not good news! But a God who welcomes penitents and graces them with forgiveness, restoration and life, that is very good news! In effect, therefore, David is saying, 'I will teach others because the truth about you is a delight and worth sharing.'[22]

So two great truths join hands in these verses. There is the sobering truth that individual sin blights the whole corporate body of the Lord's people; the sin of one is like leaven permeating a whole batch of dough.[23] The body is one, and each member has its individual responsibility for the well-being of the whole. This is true of each member, but it is crucially true of leaders, and David was aware that, as king, his sin could prove to be a corrupting, rotting virus, eating into the very fabric of his city, making its walls (verse 18) – its protective security – disintegrate. Isaiah taught this same truth in connection with the Lord's vineyard (Isaiah 5:1–7). If only the Lord's people had continued in obedience to his word, the defences of the vineyard would have been impregnable, but the foul fruit of unrighteousness provoked the Lord to 'take away its hedge … break down its wall …', and allow the beasts in to trample it to destruction (5:5). As king, David could not look on his sin as a mere 'private concern' unrelated to his public position and responsibilities.

The linked truth is one bringing the sweetest comfort. The Lord's 'Zion', the city he has chosen, is a whole company of penitent sinners,[24] accepted before God through the efficacy of the shedding of blood which he has appointed (verse 19), and living with him in the reality of the broken spirit and contrite heart of repentance (verse 17). This is the secure city of verse 18, the 'strong city' guarded by ramparts of salvation, populated by those who are righteous before their God, and who enjoy his peace through personal faith (Isaiah 26:1–4).

It is in this context that all the ordinances of God are fully effective, as the double 'then' of verse 19, which is both temporal and causal, indicates. When the Lord's people realize that the ritual of the sacrifices, as such, has no appeal for the Lord (verse 16), when they truly come to him broken and contrite,[25] 'then' (verse 19a) the sacrifices are 'righteous', that is to say 'right with God', exactly what he requires and desires, and 'then' (verse 19b) all the blessings of the altar of God – the blessings that flow from the subsititutionary offerings – are enjoyed. Repentance alone will not suffice. There must be an objective ground on which the penitent stands – the atonement made by the sacrifices the Lord has appointed. Equally, the sacrifices alone will not do; there must be personal appropriation of the Lord's grace through the wonder of repentance.

Notes

1 For a fuller diagram of this 'trajectory', see Alec Motyer, *Discovering the Old Testament* (Crossway Books, 2006), p. 95.

2 The reference in 2 Samuel 10:2 shows that Bible historians (like all historians) record only what they select as significant – even though we might want to know more! Nahash of Ammon (either David's Nahash or another king in the same royal line) had greeted Saul's

accession with a potentially savage incursion (1 Samuel 11:1-2), but David, at his best, had a real gift for getting on with people and establishing friendship.

3 2 Samuel 12:1: This is one of the very rare occasions when the historian pauses to pass a moral comment on what he records. Mostly we are left to read the story and, with the help of the rest of the Bible, draw our own conclusions.

4 1 John 1:8-9.

5 Luke 12:48.

6 Sin = ḥaṭṭā'â. The verb √ḥāṭā' means to miss the mark (compare Judges 20:16). Morally and spiritually, therefore, to fall short of what the Lord commands; to veer to one side or the other of it.

7 Psalm 32 may very well belong to this period in David's life, though the heading does not say so. Note specially verses 3-4. David went through a period of self-deception, apparently wrestling with his refusal to admit the truth, but then came to 'acknowledge' sin to God ('I let you know my sin').

8 Isaiah 43:25; Jeremiah 31:34.

9 Exodus 20:13-14; Deuteronomy 22:22; Exodus 21:12.

10 In verse 4, NIV, NRSV, 'so that', expressing consequence, should undoubtedly be 'in order that' (compare RV, NKJV), expressing purpose. If we should ever say, 'Lord, you are sovereign. Why didn't you stop me?', the Lord would reply, 'Because I purposed to bring you to recognize your sinfulness and my holiness and righteousness – to know yourself as you are and to know me as I am.' Even in our sin, for which not he but we are responsible, he, in his marvellous way, is working his purpose out.

11 This must be allowed to bear on the question of the status of the foetus, and the debate about abortion.

12 In verse 8a 'let me hear' may point to restoration to the worshipping community and the joyful songs of worship. The leper or a person defiled by contact with death was so excluded (Numbers 5:2-3; 19:11), and David would have felt deeply any such banishment from corporate enjoyment of the Lord's presence. Verse 8b, by contrast, would speak of restoration to personal wholeness and joy before God. The two halves of verse 9 deal respectively with the way our sin offends God (the hidden face), and the way it is a blot on our record ('blot out' = 'wipe away'). Sin hurts him and mars us.

13 On 'sin', 'iniquity', and 'blot out', see p. 120 above; on the physically
   debilitating consequence of sin and being at odds with God, see Psalm
   32:3-4, which could well belong to this same incident in David's life.

14 John 14:16.

15 Acts 7:51; Ephesians 4:30; 1 Thessalonians 5:19.

16 This may not be the best way to approach verse 11. David was
   obviously gripped by the most colossal conviction of sin. In such a
   state Christian believers too may well despair that the Holy One could
   possibly continue to indwell such as they, and pray against his
   departure even while they know that he will never leave them. Our
   personalities are frequently much more complicated than our
   theology, logically considered, should allow!

17 Compare John 14:16, 26: the Holy Spirit's title, *parakletos*, which the
   NIV translates by the less than enthralling word 'Counsellor', means, as
   has been often said, 'One called alongside' – i.e., called by the Father
   to stand alongside the believer (and leap to our aid).

18 Compare F. D. Kidner's remark (*Psalms 1 – 72*, Tyndale Old Testament
   Commentary, IVP, 1973, p. 193) about 'the close connection between
   a joyous faith and an infectious one ... between experiencing
   restoration (verse 12) and leading others to that knowledge (verse 13)'.

19 The emotive word 'excellencies' here is derived from 1 Peter 2:9 in the
   RV and in the *New Translation*, J. N. Darby's fine rendering of the Bible.

20 In verse 14, 'bloodguilt' is literally 'bloods'. The plural is used for 'shed
   blood', and then for the guilt incurred by shedding blood. David is
   thinking of Uriah. 'The God who saves me' is, literally, 'the God of
   my salvation', 'my saving God' – i.e., salvation is an attribute of the
   divine nature, and I have been allowed to experience it – but because
   it belongs in the heart of God it is available for all who repent. David
   goes on to write that it is the Lord's 'righteousness' that makes him
   sing. He wants his hearers to know that 'salvation' is not 'letting
   people off' by pretending sin doesn't matter. God's righteous nature
   has been satisfied; his righteous standards have been met – i.e., some
   sacrifice known to God has made propitiation and its blood has been
   sprinkled by hyssop (see verse 7).

21 Verses 18–19, says A. A. Anderson, *The Psalms* (New Century Bible,
   London, 1972), reveal an 'attitude to sacrifice different from the rest of
   the Psalm' (compare verse 16 with verse 19), and are 'often regarded as
   a later gloss of exilic or post-exilic origin, to adapt this individual psalm

for the use of the community, or to correct the false impression that God required only spiritual sacrifices'. This is self-evidently absurd. How can a psalm be 'adapted' by contradicting it? How can a community be asked to sing contradictory things? Consider a church today claiming to be Christian but denying the resurrection of Jesus. They don't want to deprive themselves of the treasures of Christian hymnody. So, at Easter, in order to continue to sing 'Hail the day that sees him rise', hey, let's add a final (adapting) verse:

> Hail the day! He did not rise!
>   In the grave his body lies.
> But the church his glory hails
>   Singing fabricated tales.

Contradiction does not 'adapt'. It just contradicts! This is not a scholarly or even a sensible way to handle the Bible. Whatever way we are to understand these concluding verses, (a) verses 16–17 suit the psalm so far. In a general way David may be pondering the fact that no sacrifice has been authorized to deal with adultery and murder. Therefore, on the sheer grounds of the grace, compassion and changeless love of the Lord (verses 1–2), the assumption is valid that there is, nevertheless, a sacrifice known to him, to be applied by hyssop (verse 7), and received through repentance. But, more exactly, in verse 16 David does not mention the 'sin offering' but the 'fellowship' or 'peace' offering (Leviticus 3) and the burnt offering (Leviticus 1) – i.e., offerings associated with a life of fellowship with God and his people, and with consecration to him respectively. This life was never a mere matter of ritual conformism but always of getting and being right with God. No correctness of sacrifice can replace or be effective without the heart and will to walk with God. (b) Verses 19 and 16 belong together around the thought of what delights the Lord and both focus on the fellowship and the burnt offerings; verses 16 and 20 share the thought of the divine 'pleasure'. There is thus in verses 16–19 both an internal unity and a satisfactory link back into the body of the psalm.

22 Compare Romans 1:16.

23 Compare 1 Corinthians 12:25–26 and 1 Corinthians 5:6–8.

24 Compare Isaiah 1:27. 'Zion' is the city where the Lord chose to set his name (Deuteronomy 12:5; Psalm 132:13), prefiguring the present 'abode'

of those who belong to Jesus (Hebrews 12:22–24), and the coming eternal city, the 'new earth' in which the redeemed will live for ever (Revelation 21:9–27).

25 'Contrite' is, literally, 'crushed'. If any distinction is to be drawn between 'broken' and 'contrite', the former suggests the end of personal power to do anything, the latter the overwhelming power ranged against us. Our powers have been broken; opposing power is a crushing weight.

Psalm 3
14 'Waking or sleeping, thy presence my light'

Background reading: 2 Samuel 13 – 15; 17 – 18

Notwithstanding the direct command of Deuteronomy 17:14–17, David pandered to his own desires and copied kings of his day in polygamy and keeping a large harem (2 Samuel 5:13). A conglomerate of many households is particularly open to divisiveness, and David's own moral collapse with Bathsheba left him unequipped to deal with sexual laxity in his extended family. When his eldest son, Amnon (2 Samuel 3:2), raped his half-sister, Absalom's full sister, Tamar (2 Samuel 13:1, 11–14), Absalom took vengeance (13:8). David gravely mishandled the ensuing crisis (e.g. 14:23–24), and this, coupled with his own implied neglect of his royal duties (15:1–5), opened the way for Absalom's rebellion (15:10).

As to why Columba left Ireland in 563 AD, some say one thing and some another, but no one questions his resoluteness and bravery as a missionary and evangelist, nor his gifts as scholar, preacher and pastor. He braved the sea and the terrors of a foreign and very hostile land to found his monastery on the tiny island of Iona, off the west coast of Scotland. Using it as his base, he journeyed often and deep into the menacing land of the Picts, bringing the gospel of Christ, and as he set off into darkness and danger he sang:

> Alone with none but thee, my God,
>   I journey on my way.
> What need I fear when thou art near,
>   O King of night and day!
> More safe am I within thy hand
>   Than if a host did round me stand.[1]

Like all the Celtic missionary monks, Columba would have been saturated with the Psalms, and who is to say that his song was not prompted by David and Psalm 3? In any case, no words could offer us a better entrance into David's mind as he moved to put the greatest possible distance between himself and his rebel son, Absalom.

That difficult word 'if'

If only David had not committed adultery with Bathsheba. If only he had been in a position to deal resolutely with his son Amnon when he raped Absalom's sister, the beautiful Tamar. If only he had not connived at the murder of Uriah, and had been able to take the moral high ground when Absalom avenged his sister and murdered Amnon. If only he had not married a heathen wife and provided a haven for Absalom to run to. If only he had been more humbly generous of heart to Absalom, less huffy, more aware of his own follies, listening to his heart instead of to his pride. If only he had been attending more efficiently to his royal duties, so that Absalom's insinuations would have carried no weight. If only!

Oh David, David! You won your laurels the hard way, but laurels are for living up to, not for resting on.

But we are never told what would have happened. We only know what *did* happen – the grimly sad unravelling of David's character (Bathsheba and Uriah), his family (Amnon and Tamar), and, finally, his kingdom, when, almost without trying, Absalom blew the trumpet of rebellion and David was faced with the major, northern three-quarters of his kingdom up in arms against him.

Flight

The story of the rebellion is one of the best bits of history-writing in the Bible (2 Samuel 15–19), full of incident, characters and deep, deep, heart-wrenching sadness, but only the early days (and nights) concern us as we study Psalm 3.

David may well have allowed a certain slackness into his planning and decision-making, and this is all too understandable. The passing years made the rigours of campaigning more demanding than they once seemed. But the old skills were still there – to Absalom's tragic cost. The news of the rebellion mobilized David in a flash, and three cardinal decisions were instantly obvious. The first was that this must be a military, not a civilian war. Jerusalem and its citizens were not going to be the front line, therefore the city must be evacuated. Mobilization was announced, and, very movingly, the king's men were at his disposal. Allied to this decision to spare Jerusalem the hardships of siege (a brave and costly decision in itself, since there was no way Absalom could have taken the city if David had chosen to defend it), was the placing of 'moles' inside Absalom's councils. Poor Absalom! His father was not the spent force he thought he was. He didn't stand a chance once he had inadvertently revitalized David! He was to discover to his cost that there was all too much life in the old dog. David's third decision was that he, not Absalom, would choose the site for the decisive battle that must be fought: he 'took to the hills', the sort of terrain where his earlier experience had honed his fighting skills.

He did not, however, head south from Jerusalem, into his old campaigning country in the southern wilderness of Judah, but east and north, seeking to put the Jordan between himself and the expected pursuit, and to give himself a breather to assemble his forces and plan the final moves. After three days' travel he reached Mahanaim, ten miles east of Jordan, across the river from the heartland of Absalom's support. It would have made sense to go south where his practised skill as a guerrilla fighter could have been deployed, but choosing Mahanaim gave notice that he intended to take the war right into 'enemy' country, and it must have struck fear into every rebel heart to realize what they were now facing. If, in addition, David felt that he would be among friends at Mahanaim, he was right.[2]

The first night out: a surprising peace

Psalm 3 suits the occasion indicated in the heading. The threefold 'many' (verses 1–2) matches the reference to the 'men of Israel' in 2 Samuel 15:13, and 'all Israel' in 17:11; the implication (Psalm 3:5–6) of the possibility of imminent attack suits 2 Samuel 17:1 – and, even without that reference, it would be a sensible supposition that Absalom would lose no time in giving chase – as, indeed, would have been the unanimous decision were it not for the intervention of David's friend Hushai the Archite (17:4–14). The widespread view that even the Lord had abandoned David (Psalm 3:2) found individual expression in the exultant Shimei.[3] In particular, verse 5 cries out to be linked with the first night of David's 'flight' from Jerusalem – strategic withdrawal would be more accurate. The subject ('I') is emphatic – just imagine this being true of me! Placed as I am! – and the verbs are past tense, looking back on a delightful, if surprising, experience: 'For my part, I went to bed, and how I slept![4] I woke up, for Yahweh himself keeps sustaining me.' This is the voice of the fine, realistic and believing David of 2 Samuel 16:10–12. Faced with Shimei's imprecations, he bows his head to the will of the sovereign God. If he meets with adversity, it is because the Lord has so directed and because it is right for that to happen; but to sleep through the night as though Absalom and his deadly pursuit did not exist, and to awake to a new day – this too is the will of the sovereign God, and lovely evidence of his sustaining hand.

So what does the psalm say?

The most obvious analysis of the Hebrew text is to see it in three stanzas, each one composed of three double lines. This almost corresponds to the verses in our Bibles.

- In verses 1–3, David is realistic about his problem. Note the threefold 'many' (verses 1–2), and, to reproduce the feeling of what he writes, repeat the 'how' of line one before the second and third occurrences of 'many'. But with equal realism (verse 3) he asserts the sufficiency of the Lord.

- In verses 4–6, David testifies that he experienced answered prayer (verse 4), and the answer was a night's sleep (verse 5), and, in the morning, a buoyant spirit ready for the day – and for the fray (verse 6). The situation has not changed, but David has!
- Finally, in verses 7–8, David looks confidently to the future. The resource of prayer is still available (verse 7a); the Lord will answer, vigorously and effectively (verse 7b).[5] Salvation[6] is the Lord's prerogative (verse 8a), and the welfare of his people (verse 8b) is safe in his hands.

This is all familiar ground in David's thinking. Granted, there had been the royal carelessness that fertilized disaffection in the northern tribes; granted, there was real colour to the opinion of 'many' (verse 2) that David had sinned grace away and was now beyond divine intervention, but David knew better. The Lord does not change, no matter what 'everybody' is saying. Humanly speaking, the scales of power are now tipped against him, but the Lord is still 'a shield around me' (verse 3); circumstances (including his own folly) have stripped him of the trappings of royal and worldly honour, but there is a glory that cannot be forfeited (verse 3): the Lord in all his glory does not desert his own. People may be saying that 'God will not deliver' (literally, 'there is no salvation for him in God'), but the king knows that his head, now bowed by sorrow and loss, will be raised in restoration (verse 3), for (verse 8) 'Salvation belongs to the LORD.'[7] It is his sovereign prerogative and gift, and, once given, it is never withdrawn.

The old remedy

This great reservoir – so to speak – of salvation which the Lord owns can be 'tapped' by prayer. This was David's experience (yet again!), and is what he would share now with us. Absalom's rebellion was, as we have seen, a pretty direct product of David's sin with Bathsheba and her husband, but, behind all that, in Absalom's own case, was David a loving but absentee father – more interested in marrying wives than in bringing up children? Is it significant that Tamar, when speaking to Amnon, refers to David not as 'our father' but as 'the king'? Maybe. But without venturing where only speculation can lead, David was in yet another mess because of his own silliness and irresponsibility. Yet the door of prayer remained ajar; the Lord's ear was open; salvation was there to be asked for. So we read, in verse 4, that 'with my voice, to the Lord, I kept crying out' (NKJV). The order of David's words is important. (1) Prayer is putting our needs into words. This is what he put first, meaning not loudness (NIV, 'aloud') but verbalization. The Lord loves to hear from us what he already knows about us – just as Jesus asked the blind man, 'What do you want me to do for you?',[8] as if the matter were in doubt and he uncertain about it! (2) Prayer is bringing our needs to the Lord. Sharing with a friend may be a relief, and loving sympathy is always welcome, even if the problem is left unsolved or the need unmet. Equally, moaning to ourselves about the toughness of our situation is always the easy course – and never does any good; in fact, by keeping the problem alive in our minds it may make it loom even larger. The effective thing is to 'take it to the Lord in prayer'. (3) Prayer is persistent. David 'kept' crying out. This is what the Lord Jesus will call the 'knocking' aspect of prayer in Matthew 7:7. 'Asking' is the simplicity of prayer; 'seeking' is the discipline of prayer; 'knocking' is the persistence of prayer, until the great Friend (Luke 11:5) rises and takes our need upon himself.

In contrast with David's 'keeping on' asking, the Lord 'answered'. His moment came, and he acted, definitely, precisely.[9] The reference to the 'holy hill' is important. It is there to remind us to whom we are speaking and of whom we are asking. The confidence with which we are allowed to come must never degenerate into arrogance. It is those who know their need of mercy who can come with boldness; the throne is a 'throne of grace', but it is still a throne; confident and welcome, we enter through the blood of Jesus, but it is still 'the Holy Place' into which we come.[10] That is one side of the meaning of the reference to the 'holy hill'. Another side is this, that although the Lord is the 'high and lofty One ... whose name is holy' (Isaiah 57:15), and is therefore grossly offended by our sinful ways, yet he, in all his holiness, still welcomes, awaits, hears and answers our prayer. And still another side is this, that Absalom thought that he had become master of Zion's hill, but the Lord had not abdicated; David had been driven from his throne but the Lord was still on the throne. No power of man, no cleverly drawn design, no sin, fault or failing – nothing can alter the single simple fact of a sovereign, reigning, holy God, rich in love to all who call upon him (Psalm 86:5).

What surpassing thoughtfulness and gentle, understanding love was expressed in the first tokens of answered prayer! David does not tell us in what words he 'kept calling' on the Lord. He must surely have put the downfall of Absalom and his own restoration at the forefront, whatever else he asked, but we cannot be wrong in thinking that what he was given was something he never even thought of asking for, or, perhaps, never felt to be a particular need: a good night's sleep (verse 5)! It was only in retrospect that he realized that the Lord was in this, that a night's sleep, in those circumstances, was in itself something of a miracle of divine working, and that his consequent refreshed and improved sense of well-being was in fact at that moment exactly the right answer (verse 6).[11] When we pray, every next thing that happens is the start of the Lord's reply.

What a prayer to pray!

Does verse 7 reveal the terms of David's prayers in verse 4, or does it tell us how he put to use the new-found energies that his night's sleep gave him (verse 6)? Probably both. It is reasonable, on the one hand, to think that his prayers would have been preoccupied with his own deliverance and the overthrow of his opponents. It is striking and instructive, on the other hand, to think that new energies resulted in a fresh engagement in prayer. That is as it should be. It would have been very easy for David to allow this exhilaration and buoyancy of spirit (verse 6) to lead into self-reliance and the confidence of an experienced soldier that he would soon deal himself with this upstart threat! But no. The resource is still prayer – not personal ability, or even 'gift'. Only the Lord is sufficient. The victory can be only his. So prayer is the thing, not only when we are 'down' (verses 1–2 leading into verses 3–4), but also when we are 'up' (verses 5–6 leading into verse 7). This is by far the most important thing to learn from verses 5–7.

But – we must ask – what about the violent way David put his prayer into words? It is one thing to request prompt ('arise'[12]) and effective ('deliver/save') divine action, but it is surely quite another thing actually to specify a knockout blow ('on the jaw') of such force that teeth are broken![13] Is this a proper way to pray?

'Imprecations' – prayers calling for disaster to befall others – are not unknown in the Psalms. There are, in fact, between thirty-five and forty occurrences of prayers that, to say the least, sound odd to us – and, at the worst, seem downright sinful.[14] Psalm 144:11-12 is an instructive case in point. We would readily pray, 'Preserve my life . . . bring me out of trouble', but baulk at ' . . . destroy my foes . . . ' In other words, we find it acceptable to pray 'bland' prayers, but stop short of saying out loud (or even admitting inwardly) what those prayers actually involve if they are to be answered in the practicalities of life as it is today. For cases are not hard to find in which the deliverance of one can happen only through the downfall of another. The Bible is more realistic. Where we leave implications unsaid, the Bible puts them into words; where we shelter behind innocuous requests, the Bible makes their implications also part of the way it prays.

It must have broken David's heart to pray verse 7b, knowing that the answer would come at a heavy cost to his beloved Absalom. But prayer leaves the outcome in the hands of the Lord, the only place where it can be left with safety.

The wider picture

It was not only Absalom, however, whose fate would have broken David's heart – and struck deep into his conscience as well. Certainly he did not create Absalom's rebellion, nor did he compel anyone to be associated with it, but in a deeper sense it was all his fault. He was the king! It was his laxity that allowed fault lines to become fissures, and petty grievances to become critical national issues. Absalom had the material of rebellion handed to him on a plate. Yet David is still king, and the future has to be faced. Very well, then. Put it into the Lord's hands, for 'salvation belongs to the LORD' (verse 8a, NKJV) and he alone can bring the blessing the whole people need (verse 8b). How easily David could have ended this psalm with 'on me [be] your blessing'! Or 'on us' – the faithful band around him in his flight. But his heart goes out to all: to those who have accepted the cost of following him;

doubtless to the Jerusalemites whom his resolute decision saved from the horrors of a siege; and also to the men of Israel who had rallied to Absalom's banner – 'They are all your people, Lord. Please bless them.' David had jeopardized the future, but in this too the door of prayer was ajar and the Lord's ear open. 'If we are faithless, he will remain faithful, for he cannot disown himself.'[15]

Notes

1 See *Irish Church Hymnal* (Dublin, 1936), number 350.

2 2 Samuel 17:27–29. Possibly the occasion prompting Psalm 23: see especially Psalm 23:5.

3 2 Samuel 16:7–8. Anderson (see Chapter 13, note 21) wonders if Zion was called 'Yahweh's holy hill' (Psalm 3:4) in David's time – to which the sufficient reply is 'Why not?' He also finds it a problem that Absalom is not mentioned by name – which is a misunderstanding of the way these Davidic meditations on 'the story within the story' operate. Contrast this with Van Gemeren, *Psalms*, The Expositor's Bible, Vol. 5 (Zondervan, 1991): 'There is no internal evidence that brings into doubt the authenticity of the superscription.'

4 The verb is in an emphatic form. The emphasis could be just on the fact of sleep in such circumstances of discomfort and anxiety; it could be, as above, on the quality of the sleep enjoyed.

5 The second half of verse 7 can be given different emphases. The verbs 'strike ... break' are in the perfect tense, which the NIV has chosen to interpret as imperatives. They are more likely to be 'perfects of certainty', i.e., future acts so certain to be accomplished that they may be spoken of as having happened already. This can be expressed by a translation such as 'For you have determined to strike' or 'For you are sure to strike.' The NIV, as so often, omits the initial 'for', which explains the confidence on which 'arise ... deliver' (literally, 'save') in verse 7a depend.

6 Verse 8, literally, 'To Yahweh belongs salvation; upon his people [is, comes, rests] his blessing'. Note how, as in Psalm 51, the king cannot fail to consider the national aspect of the situation – which David knows is implicated in his own.

7 NIV 'deliver' (verse 2) and 'deliverance' (verse 8) are, literally, in each case 'salvation'. They form the 'bracket' round the psalm, the

framework within which it operates. This is its controlling thought, while its central thought is expressed in verses 4–6.

8 Matthew 6:8; 20:32.

9 The verb 'answered' is in the perfect tense, used here to express decisiveness but not necessarily promptness, as *we* think of promptness! Prayer never goes unanswered, but the answer may be 'no', 'not yet' or 'not quite that', until the divine 'now' arrives.

10 Hebrews 4:14–16; 10:19.

11 Compare 1 Kings 19:4–6. Elijah thought he needed sudden death; the Lord knew he needed a night's sleep and breakfast in bed!

12 David's cry 'Arise' recalls Moses' word (Numbers 10:35). By using this great cry, David expressed his confidence that his small, fleeing company was in fact the onward march of the Lord's people with the Lord at their head.

13 Striking the cheek is a sign of insult (1 Kings 22:24); breaking the teeth is rendering harmless, making the tiger toothless.

14 E.g. Psalms 69; 109. See A. Motyer, 'Psalms', in the *New Bible Commentary*, 21st Century Edition (IVP, 1994), p. 488; *The Story of the Old Testament* (Candle Books, 2001), pp. 71–72; *Discovering the Old Testament* (Crossway Books, 2006), pp. 116–117.

15 2 Timothy 2:13.

Psalm 63

15 Weary days, sleepless nights: a God for all seasons

Background reading: 2 Samuel 17

It was a brave and self-sacrificing decision on David's part to evacuate Jerusalem. He saved the city from siege, but exposed himself to what he surely must have thought a thing of the past – a life on the run, a return to the wilderness and maybe even the caves. On the second night 'out' he faces the grim prospect of the future.

If David thought that his second night on the run would be a replica of the first, he was wrong.

He was not to know that on that first, dangerous night, though well within reach of Absalom's pursuit, he was in fact, by divine overruling, totally safe. Be that as it may. Morning light not only found him refreshed and ready for the day (Psalm 3:5–6), but also brought him inside news of Absalom's plans, and an urgent directive to put the Jordan between himself and the rebels without delay. It took another day and night to achieve this, and, as it happened, it was not a moment too soon, for as David reached Mahanaim, with its friendly welcome and thoughtful care, Absalom too crossed the Jordan with his full force of fighting men, and set up camp in Gilead.

It was obviously a pretty close-run thing: on the one hand, David, slowed down as he must have been by the mixed nature of his company, and on the other, the speedy forced march of which Absalom's militia would have been capable.

It is about that second day's march and second night out that David meditates in Psalm 63. The atlases show that 'the wilderness of Judah' (Psalm 63, heading) extended along the western shore of the Dead Sea and then northwards along the Jordan. We do not know where David forded the river, but, wherever it was, the equally unwelcoming east bank awaited him, and the long desert haul north and east to Mahanaim – and (so I am told) those who have not been there simply cannot appreciate what such a journey means. The aridity of the terrain was matched by the energy-sapping thirst of the traveller in stifling heat – 'a dry and weary land', indeed, 'where there is no water' (verse 1), coupled with the fact that though night-time brought welcome shade, it did not this time bring the balm of sleep (verse 6). Consequently, as we read his psalm, we find ourselves listening to the travel-weary, sleepless voice of the king as he faces – and yet marvellously outfaces – the unwelcome pressures of the change from comfort to discomfort, palace to earthen couch, city amenity to wilderness want, and security to life-threatening enmity (verse 9).

The missing word

We could be forgiven for thinking that David would automatically – indeed, with good reason – say 'Why?' Why is God's chosen, anointed king (Psalm 89:19–20; 1 Samuel 16:13) a hunted fugitive? Why have the divine promises (Psalm 89:32–34) turned sour? Why, indeed?

Not that the question 'Why?' is necessarily wrong. Jesus asked 'Why?' (Matthew 27:46, quoting Psalm 22:1). But 'Why?' was not where the Lord Jesus started. His first word was 'My God' – in other words, his 'Why?' was in the context of undiminished faith, whereas when we ask 'Why?' we are usually expressing doubt about whether the Lord really is our God, whether he really cares, and whether he really is sovereign.

David shows us the better way, the way to face changed circumstances, ill fortune and human hostility with resolute faith. It can be expressed simply. In Psalm 3, as we saw, David's resource was 'Take it to the Lord in prayer.' In Psalm 63, in the same trouble, enduring the same adversities, facing the same desert and fearing the same foes, he asks nothing. The whole thrust of the psalm is just to recall all that is known about the Lord, to keep him in mind, to covet and enjoy his presence, to affirm and reaffirm the truth, and to rejoice in God. Read the psalm through and discover that this is indeed so!

The true question to ask is not 'Why?' but 'Who?' This is the question that changes the focus of attention from the misery of personal experience to the God of grace and glory, the God of all power and might. The question 'Who?' does not soothe the misery away, but it does soothe the troubled spirit, pointing to the majestic God who is truly God, the God in charge, the God who orders all things according to the perfection of his own just, wise and loving will. For what bothers us in times of trouble is our sense of purposelessness. We just can't see the point, but this is why the Bible assures us that 'he guides me in paths of righteousness for his name's sake' (Psalm 23:3), that is to say, paths that make sense to him, that conform to all that his name means, and which fulfil the good pleasure of his will.

David's affirmations; our objectives

It is in this frame of mind that we meet David in Psalm 63, opening his mind to us as he faces a painful present and an uncertain future. He is our teacher in anticipation of the day when we need to learn the lessons he imparts. The psalm sets out four great principles.

(1) In a stressful time, our first objective is not to change our circumstances but to seek after our God (verse 1).
The psalm sounds as if it came naturally to David to respond to his difficulties in this way. He was facing and enduring what he calls 'a dry and weary land'. The word 'weary' really means 'fainting' or 'expiring'. We know how plants wilt without water. The very land-scape before him was 'wilting' – and David and his company would likewise find their whole physical being 'wilting', fainting away, dehydrated and dying. Of course they would have made provision for all this, by securing some sort of water supply, but that is not what

David is sharing with us. He wants us to know that the first reaction to hostility and adversity is not to counter it or seek to change it, but to make it a model for our walk with God – to long for him as thirsty people long for water, and to 'seek' him as thirsty people make for a well! He wants us to make sure that our spiritual needs (and their satisfaction in God) are every bit as real to us as whatever physical or circumstantial need we may have at any given moment.

How very far this is from the questions with which we can so easily bombard God when suffering comes! It is actually the very opposite of retreating and holding off from God, which so often is our first reaction. In his 'dry and weary land' David is a man of unshaken faith. He says, 'O God, you are my God.' The two nouns lie side by side in the Hebrew – 'O God, my God.' The former points to the God who is God indeed, the One who possesses and exercises all the divine attributes and powers; the second is God the transcendent, the God who is over all, through all and in all, and David asserts his personal faith – even though none of his problems has yet been solved – by the simplicity of the possessive pronoun 'my'. The word translated (by the NIV) as 'earnestly seek' appears in other versions (e.g. NKJV) as 'early seek', and this meaning is certainly the more obvious, and (at the least) not to be resisted: David greeted the troubled and trouble-some day with an affirmation of faith in his great and sovereign God (verse 1a), with a first-thing-in-the-morning session alone with God (verse 1b), and with a determination that his spiritual needs should be his paramount objectives (verse 1cd) – a recipe for us for troubled days.

(2) Question: Are we using the present to store up lessons and experiences of God for the future (verses 2–5)? For the Lord does not change, and what he has proved to be in the past he can be trusted to be at every point of our pilgrimage.

Places and situations change; the Lord does not! David looks back on meeting God 'in the sanctuary' (verse 2), and recalls how this prompted praise (verse 3). But the same Lord is present all the time and in every place; therefore altered circumstances, as far as that is concerned, make no difference. His name is still the same; therefore the way of praise can still be followed (verse 4), and the satisfactions that a praising fellowship with God brings can still be enjoyed (verse 5).

These few verses of the psalm are a little more complicated – and a bit more telling – than the NIV makes them. They centre on a comparison of past and present:

v. 2   Just as, in the sanctuary,[1] I caught the vision of you,
        in respect of seeing your power and your glory –

v. 3   (for better is your changeless love than life:
        my lips praise you) –

v. 4   So I will bless you as long as I live;
        in your name I will lift up my hands;[2]

v. 5   as with fatness and richness my soul will be satisfied,
        and with loud-sounding lips my mouth will praise you.

In Psalm 34:1 David called us to 'bless the LORD at all times' (NKJV), and here we see that he practised what he preached. Wilderness or no wilderness, thirst or no thirst, fainting or no fainting, praise filled his mouth. It is in this connection that the reference to the Lord's 'name' is significant, for this is the unchanging reality of the believer's life. The name declares, and is a constant reminder of, who and what the Lord is. For this reason we always have a cause for praise: Jesus is the same; salvation is the same; eternal life and security are the same. Even in the direst circumstances the door of worship lies open, and we are called to 'bless the LORD' – to review the wonders and glories of his nature and to respond in wonder, love and praise.

The particular thrust of verses 2–5, however, is that, in David's case, the past nourished and undergirded the present. Because he practised the presence of God when the 'sanctuary' in the city of David was available to him, he had a stored-up spirituality on which to draw when the external facilities and comforts were withdrawn. He experienced the reality of what the Lord Jesus teaches in the story of the ten bridesmaids – all the girls had flickering lamps, but the 'wise' ones were distinguished from the 'foolish' by also having oil in store.[3]

Today is the Lord's intended preparation for tomorrow. To miss or mishandle today's seeking after God – in the place of prayer; in reading and pondering his Word, in personal or corporate worship, in fellowship, at the Lord's Table – is to send ourselves naked and vulnerable into the demands of the future.

(3) The difficult patches of life summon us to concentration, commitment and trust (verses 6–8).

Though the Lord never changes, his dealings with us cannot be presumed. As on only the previous night David had reported that 'I lay down and slept; I woke again, because the Lord was sustaining me' (Psalm 3:5), on his second night of flight he might well have expected a repeat experience, but it was not to be so. Now the night watches were wakeful, even though the Lord who sustained him was still there to help (verses 6–7).

So how did David spend his sleepless hours, and to what does his example call and encourage us? To remembrance (verse 6), gladness (verse 7), and rest in God (verse 8).

Years before, David, all alone, had looked up into the black vault of the cave in which he was hiding and seen the overshadowing wings of his God (Psalm 57, heading and verse 1). Now, wide awake under the canopy of the night sky, faith sees the same wings (verse 7), and, even if sleep eludes him, the spirit is at rest. He has food for the mind (verse 6), a song for the lips (verse 7), and a bedtime companion (verse 8). 'Remembering' calls the past to the aid of the present; 'thinking' draws out the lessons, and dwells on the truths already learnt, and both together make the Lord's presence a contemporary reality – 'you are my help'. Did David actually burst into song (verse 7b)? Not a popular move in the middle of the night, though not unknown (see Acts 16:25) – and the verb translated 'sing' does mean 'sing aloud'! But there is a song in the heart that resounds like the loudest singing within the one who is caught up in the presence of the Lord and the joy he brings. Consequently, David went from remembrance, pondering a song – there and then, wakeful ... endangered ... whatever – to clinging even more firmly to the God who was upholding him (verse 8). David clings; the Lord grips. Maybe he would allow us to put it like this, that the more determinedly he clung, the closer he 'stuck' to the Lord, and the more aware he was of the grip of that great encircling hand.[4]

(4) Keep the lamp of hope shining brightly. What the Lord has promised he will most surely keep and perform (verses 9–11).

'Hope' is nowadays a word with a great deal of inbuilt uncertainty. We 'hope' it will be a fine day for the wedding – but the word carries no assurance. In the Bible, however, the element of uncertainty touches only the time of fulfilment, never the fulfilment itself. Thus we enjoy the hope of the imminent return of the Lord Jesus Christ: the fact is certain. It is the 'sure and certain' hope of his coming. The time is, to us, hidden; only the Father knows it.[5] This is the significance of the fact that David suddenly speaks of himself as 'the king' in verse 11. Discomfort, sleeplessness, hard times, looming danger – nothing can change the fact that the Lord has made promises to him. Marvellously (as we have seen), he came to the throne solely by divine appointment and sovereign management; not at all by personal effort, or by the raised hand of rebellion or by underhand craftiness, and now he can retain (and regain) his throne only on the same terms, but he knows that he will, for the word of the Lord is a sure word. All those who oppose the Lord's will as expressed in his word will come to nothing (verses 9–10).

The firmness and determination of David's grasp on the hope that is set before him can be measured by his gritty acknowledgment of the forces against him, and their deadly intentions. They are after his life itself. 'The dark shadow', says Kidner, 'brings out the solidity of his faith, which has nothing "fugitive and cloistered" about it.'[6] Thank God for such hard-nosed realism! David was up against it, and his example speaks directly to any and all troubles that assail the Lord's people. In the dark day, David set the lamp of hope firmly on its bracket, and the darkness could not overcome it.

David's royal future is secure (verse 11a); to grasp hold of what the Lord has revealed about himself ('God's name', verse 11b) and to let this lovely revelation draw out our full loyalty ('swear by' him, verse 11b) is the way to live with adversity, and ultimately to come through all adversities to praise. The word of the Lord, not the word of people (however seemingly dominant), will triumph (verse 11c). To hope in God, resting on his word of promise, is our ultimate resource in the day of distress.

Notes

1 Or 'in holiness'. The same possibilities occur, e.g., in Psalm 150:1, the word (*qōdeš*) referring either to the place where the holy Lord lives or to his holy nature.

2 The 'name' summarizes all that the Lord has revealed about himself. David no longer has the 'sanctuary', but the truth about the Lord has not changed.

3 Matthew 25:1–13; compare verse 4.

4 John 10:28–29.

5 Mark 13:32.

6 F. D. Kidner, *Psalms 1 – 72*, Tyndale Old Testament Commentary (IVP, 1973), p. 226.

2 Samuel 23:1–7
16 Another tale of two kings

Background reading: 2 Samuel 23; 1 Chronicles 29; 1 Kings 2

In the proverbial words, David's kingship went up like a rocket and came down like a stick. The record of his decline in 1 Kings 1 – 2 is almost too sad to read. Yet the 'real' David was still there. We do not know when he penned his 'last words' (2 Samuel 23:1), but it is pleasing to think that the weakness, disabilities and errors of his final years were offset by continuing and vibrant spirituality and expectation.

David made three wills. Firstly, he left his personal fortune for the building and adornment of the house of the Lord that his son Solomon was to build (1 Chronicles 29:3–5). Secondly – and sadly – he bequeathed to Solomon some items of unfinished business, mainly of a particularly bloodthirsty and vengeful (not to say dishonourable and promise-breaking) nature – a terrible and needless blot, actually, on David's legacy (1 Kings 2:5–6, 8–9).

But what a man of contrasts he was! His third 'last will and testament' is the gem of a poem in 2 Samuel 23. It shows all the poetic skill and mastery of words that we have seen in David's psalms, but it also bears the marks of extreme old age, and the way the elderly mind so easily tires! The high measure of allusiveness in these verses is best explained in this way, as though the aged king knew well what he wanted to say, but, having put the essence of it on paper, lacked concentration to develop the thoughts that were so characteristic of him, important for his dynasty, and precious to us.

He died looking forward. If he perhaps regretted his own failure to be the promised king, yet in his last words he revelled in the certainty that the one whom he had called 'his Lord' (Psalm 110:1) would yet come, and put everything right. The verses offer a compelling final sight of David, and allow us, with him, to fix our eyes on the coming glory of his Son and our Lord.

David's words, God's words

David's last psalm is, as we shall see as we trace its course, in three sections.

It begins (verses 1b–3a) with as clear a claim to divine inspiration as the Old Testament contains anywhere, but, as always, it deals only with the fact of inspiration, not with the way in which it came about. Every time the prophets uttered their trademark words, 'Thus says the LORD', they were registering the same claim that David makes here: what they were saying was exactly what the Lord himself would have said had he chosen to speak without their mediation. It is important to observe that David here claims inspiration not simply for his 'last words' but for his career as 'Israel's singer of songs'. It is a retrospective claim, touching all the psalms we have studied. They, just as much as David's last words, are the word of God.

David tells us eight things about himself, four public facts and four secret realities.

Here are the four public facts (verse 1):

- First, he is David, son of Jesse, that is, a veritable human being with a human ancestry;
- secondly, he holds a high position, not by his own power: he has 'been raised' (NKJV) to the heights;
- thirdly, he is the anointed king;
- and, fourthly, he is an author and composer of note.[1]

These are four 'ordinary' facts. Their sum and substance is David's human nature and human experience. Some of them make him notable. But none of these things makes him more than a man among men. They do, however, raise the question of how this David – so plainly human even if specially important and talented – can claim to speak an 'oracle', that is, a word from God couched in words from God.

The second set of four facts (verses 2–3a) answers the question:

- First (verse 2a), the Holy Spirit inspired David;
- yet, secondly (verse 2b), David was still the speaker, using the tongue God gave him;
- thirdly, the word was actually God's word, spoken by Israel's God himself (verse 3a);
- and, fourthly, it was to David personally that Israel's Rock spoke (verse 3b).[2]

The Word: fully divine, truly human

There is nothing here to tell us how the Holy Spirit goes about the task of communicating the word of God and inspiring his chosen agents to receive and speak it. All we are told is that two distinct 'realities' come together: there is the voice of the Holy Spirit revealing (verse 2a), and there is the human tongue speaking on earth what has first been spoken from heaven (verse 2b). The Holy Spirit brought David into a speaking fellowship with himself – he 'spoke with (NIV 'through') me'. But when David consequently spoke, it was not as a tape recorder. He spoke with his own 'tongue', with his own authentic voice.

We are never told how this 'miracle' happens, but all through the Bible we see the practical outcome. Bible writers claim (and rightly so) that what they say is what God is saying, but nevertheless they use the vocabulary that is naturally theirs, write or speak in their own individual styles, couch their message in their own favourite words, and offer the product of their own painstaking thought and research. Isaiah, Jeremiah, Ezekiel and the rest all say, 'Thus says the LORD', but there is no way Isaiah's 'style' could be confused with Jeremiah's, and the same is true of all the prophets.

We want to ask how the same word can be both fully divine and truly human. We do not know the answer to that question, but we do know this: the closer a person comes to God, the more truly human and, indeed, distinctively individual that person becomes. According to the Bible, their individuality is not 'lost' or submerged or absorbed into God; rather, they are 'found'; they become more really and truly themselves than they ever were before. So it was with David too. Brought into a speaking fellowship with God, he then became the truly authentic David.

The Word: God's favour, strength, and provision

Moving on to verse 3a, we learn that the Word, which God revealed by his Spirit and which, by the same Spirit, he inspired his chosen agents – in this case, David – to receive and to communicate, has three functions: it is a visible sign of his special relationship with us, and it is his provision for our security and the means of our nourishment.

First, then, it is as 'the God of Israel' that the Lord spoke to David (verse 3a) – 'Israel', whom he nominated as his firstborn son, his redeemed, his personal, treasured possession, the loved and chosen object of his covenanted mercies, and now the Israel of God, the blessed, worldwide company of all who believe in Jesus.[3] Our loving God desires to speak to us personally, to tell us of himself, to instruct us in the way he would have us go, to let us know what is well pleasing to him. His Word – now not just what he shared with David but the completed volume of the holy Scriptures – is our personal and domestic 'means of grace' through which 'morning by morning' we can sit with the God of Israel while he opens our ears to hear.[4] The Father, Lord of heaven and earth, thus ministers in love to his children.[5]

When David goes on to say that it is as 'the Rock' that God spoke to him (verse 3b), he introduces further riches, a great pair consisting of the divinely intended benefits of possessing and hearing God's Word. The mere image of 'the Rock' suggests stability and security: a strong place of refuge in a time of stress (Psalm 18:1–2), a secure place when the storm rages (Psalm 61:2). But 'the Rock' also always has that special meaning that derives from Exodus 17, the 'smitten Rock' from which came water to nourish, revive and save Israel from death. God the Rock is always the nourisher and life-giver, and it is as such that he gives his people his Word. Just as the Word of God ministers to us his love, and fosters our special relationship with him as God of Israel, so also, as the gift of our Rock, it both ministers security and imparts his life and strength for our daily needs.

The king and the royal house (verses 3b–5)

David now turns to another topic, in verses of high poetry, very succinct and as richly allusive as poetry can be. Thoughts are sketched rather than developed; words and phrases lie side by side, inviting us to ponder and work out their relationship. Yet, over all, the movement and meaning of the verses are plain: David foresees the coming of the Ruler of the world, and pictures his character and influence (verses 3b–4); then he goes on to affirm with satisfaction the part his royal line is to play in respect of this great future (verse 5).

As literally as possible, the section runs like this:[6]

3b One ruling (over) mankind: Righteous!
   One ruling: the fear of God!
4 And like the light of morning
   – the sun rises –
   a morning free of clouds!
   Out of brightness, out of rain,
   green growth from the earth!
5 Indeed, is not my house so with God?
   For an eternal covenant he has put in place for me,
       set out in full and guaranteed –
   Indeed, my full salvation, and every delight –
   indeed – will he not cause it to sprout up?

When his death was near, Jacob said, 'I am about to die, but God will be with you and take you back to the land...' Joseph likewise: 'I am about to die. But God will surely come to your aid and take you up out of this land to the land he promised...'[7] Hebrews (11:13) speaks of these and many more when it says that they 'were still living by faith when they died. They did not receive the things promised; they only saw them and welcomed them from a distance.' And so it was with David. He bequeathed to Solomon some unfinished business that would have been better left unshared and unfinished, but here, in dying, he allows us to know that his own inner – and, we assume, final – preoccupation was with the ultimate future, the great unfinished business of the coming of the world-Ruler yet to be born within his dynasty. He died, not having seen the promise kept, but confident that the Word of God cannot fail.

It was surely from these 'last words' of David that Isaiah learned how to envisage the King who was yet to be (Isaiah 11:1–10) and to foresee the blessed world over which he would reign, but David learned it by direct inspiration from God. What a privilege is ours, then, as we listen to God the Holy Spirit describing God the Son in his character and work as the son of David – the glorious King whose coming again we await!

- In character, he is the Righteous One, wholly right with God, totally as God would have him be;
- in every aspect of conduct and government, he is motivated by the fear of God;
- his presence among his people is like the most perfect new day imaginable, sunshine on a fresh and cloudless morning;
- and his effect is to cause everything that is good and right to flourish and grow.

As he thus looks forward, David knows that his 'house' is central to the fulfilment of the Lord's promises, for the great, transcendent God has put in place a covenanted promise, whose provisions are fully detailed and each guaranteed by divine oath (compare Psalm 89:3–4; Hebrews 6:13), and it is the function of the 'house of David' to be the bearer of those promises until they are fulfilled. To David, however, this is more than a truth about remote descendants. It is 'my salvation and delight', his enjoyment of personal welfare, fulfilment and joy. Isaiah foresaw Jacob delighting in the still-to-come prosperity of his children;[8] David expected to be 'there' to enjoy the advent of the King.

Throughout his psalms David has been teaching us how to live. In his 'last words' he teaches us how to die: with our eyes filled with the person, presence, light, life, royal glory and confident expectation of Jesus.

Sad realism (verses 6–7)

David's last words to Solomon certainly left much to be desired, but the one thing they did not lack was realism. The heartless ruthlessness of Joab would sully the coming reign. Equally, the thoughtful devotion of Barzillai stood at the other end of the pendulum swing from the embittered hatred of Shimei. Solomon must deal appropriately with these matters. In the same way, if the ultimate kingdom is to be as undefiled as its King is righteous, there will have to be a final settlement of every opposing force. Those who will not have this man to reign over them cannot be allowed to remain.[9]

This is the sad realism that was given poetic expression in David's final poem, but in a purer form and with a higher motive than his last will and testament to Solomon. The King must reign and all his enemies must be put under his feet;[10] his angel agents will weed out of his kingdom everything that causes sin and all who do evil.[11] Of course it is true that when he comes again every knee will bow and every tongue confess that Jesus Christ is Lord,[12] but for some it will be an enforced, unwilling bowing before his overwhelming glory, and a grudging confession that is no more than an acknowledgment of missed opportunities, and a grim realization of a lost eternity. David's last words end on this deeply solemn note:

> 6 But Belial?
> Like thorns, thrown out, all of them!
> For not by hand can they be taken:
> 7 anyone who touches them
> must be wholly equipped with iron, and a spear-handle!
> And in the fire they will be burned to ashes on the spot!
> (my translation)

The word 'Belial' is found nearly thirty times in the Old Testament. It is made up of two words, *bĕlî*, meaning 'not', and *yāʿal*, meaning 'worth, profit'. In his last words, David just throws it down on the paper as an exclamation – whatever is contrary to the true God, deviates from his revealed laws, falls below his standards of integrity and obligation; what the Lord Jesus in Matthew 13 called the weeds among the wheat. For, sadly and grimly, the fact is that sinners perish along with their sin, and the words of our gentle and loving Saviour confirm the words of his greatest ancestor.

Such things and people are 'thorns', too dangerous to be touched by humans. According to Jesus, angel hands will see to this exercise; David deals only with the bare fact: those who cut down the thorns for the fire will have to be properly armed or equipped for the task, with iron-shod, long-handled tools. But, as to the outcome, there is no appeal to a higher court, nor any stay of execution. All is done 'on the spot'.

As F. D. Kidner points out in his elegant and perceptive commentary on Genesis,[13] 'the first doctrine to be denied' was 'judgment', and 'if modern denials of it are very differently motivated, they are equally at odds with revelation'. It is one of those things, unmistakably clear in Scripture, that sensitive minds would prefer not to be there. But it is, and when David laid down his pen for the last time it was on this truth of an adverse eternal destiny that he ended his inspired literary career. We who have gratefully learned so much from him as we have read his autobiography dare not cross out his dying testimony, for it, too, was spoken by the Spirit of the Lord, the God and Rock of Israel. Yes, the King is coming; and, yes, his character, presence and influence will be glorious; but, yes, also, 'that day will bring about the destruction of the heavens by fire, and the elements will melt in the heat. But in keeping with his promise we are looking forward to a new heaven and a new earth'[14] – and there the true David, the David who was always the divine intention, will reign as King for ever![15]

Notes

1 With 'exalted by the most High' the NIV goes beyond what the Hebrew text says, which is 'raised to the height'. Why does David attribute his anointing to 'the God of Jacob' specifically? Probably to point to his own lowliness (compare 2 Samuel 7:8) and even unworthiness, for the 'God of Jacob' is the God who bothers with

people like Jacob, the undeserving and unworthy. David's anointing was for the position and functions of kingship (1 Samuel 16:13) and carried no implication of inspiration of speech. 'Israel's singer of songs' is, literally, 'the delightful/the most delightful (man) in respect of the songs of Israel', compare RV (margin note): 'the pleasantest in the songs of Israel', i.e., Israel's sweetest psalmist, specifying a 'human' poetic talent.

2 In verse 2a 'through me' is better understood as 'spoke with me'. In verse 3b 'to me' is emphatic – David's sense of wonder at the voice of God coming actually to him!

3 See Exodus 4:22; 19:4–5; Isaiah 43:1; Deuteronomy 7:7–8; Galatians 3:6–7; 6:16.

4 Isaiah 50:4.

5 Matthew 11:25.

6 See also D. R. Davis, 2 Samuel: Out of Every Adversity (Christian Focus, 1999), p. 244.

7 Genesis 48:21; 50:24.

8 Isaiah 29:22–23. Not 'when they see' (NIV), but 'when he sees' (RV, NKJV, NRSV, ESV).

9 Luke 19:14, 27.

10 1 Corinthians 15:25.

11 Matthew 13:41.

12 Philippians 2:9–11.

13 F. D. Kidner, Genesis, Tyndale Old Testament Commentaries (IVP, 1967), p. 68, on Genesis 3:4.

14 2 Peter 3:12–13.

15 Ezekiel 34:22–24.

9 781844 741939